GIFFORDS CIRCUS

GIFFORDS CIRCUS

THE FIRST TEN YEARS

NELL GIFFORD

The History Press

For Toti

Frontispiece: Illustration by Lydia Gifford.

Right: Illustration by Nell Gifford.

First published 2014

The History Press
The Mill, Brimscombe Port
Stroud, Gloucestershire, GL5 2QG
www.thehistorypress.co.uk

British Library Cataloguing in Publication Data.
A catalogue record for this book is available from the British
Library.

ISBN 978 0 7524 8918 6

Typesetting and origination by The History Press
Designed by Katie Beard

Printed in India

CONTENTS

A NOTE ON OUR LOGO

This is a drawing that my mother gave me when I was 17. I love it and I think that it encapsulates the spirit of Giffords Circus.

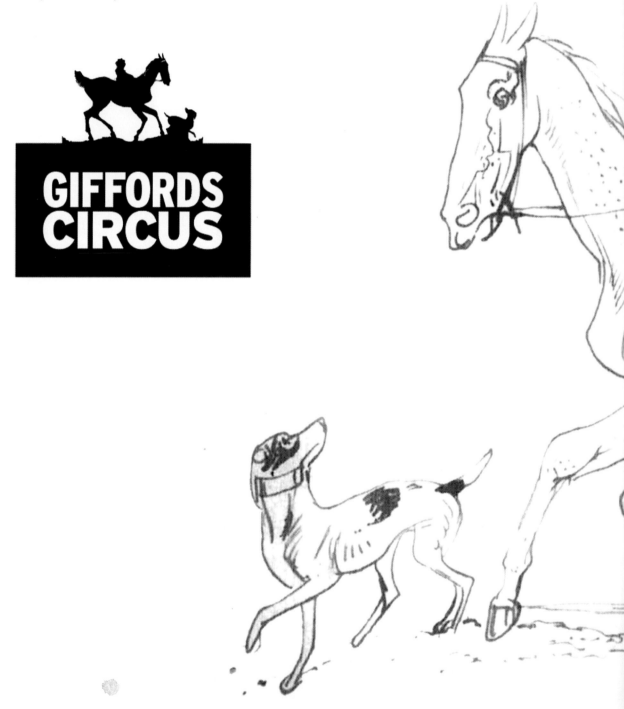

1

LET THE PLAY BEGIN

When I see a show I don't want to just be amused or moved – I want to cry. I think that a good circus should make you cry. Furthermore, a good circus, a circus that is doing its job, should somehow feel like a moment of crisis, like it is on the very brink of extinction, as if a moment of excess and brilliance has been reached and over reached. A good circus is a sublimely existential thing, living acutely and only for the golden present moment. This is what I have discovered.

I feel that I am always at the moment of being extinguished, that the thing is going to vanish, and yet it doesn't. It keeps opening up, there is always another bend in the road that I can't see around; when I get further, I find more circuses, and all I can see is that; more shows, more circuses, or something that was a circus but is now somehow different and yet more of a circus than I could ever have wished for, a circus that I did dream of, a circus to make a pilgrimage for: Giffords Circus. I can't get away from it, it chases me and I chase it, and I love it.

I am going to try and start at the beginning. I am 18 years old and I am in a circus

A good circus is a sublimely existential thing, living acutely and only for the golden present moment.

in America. I am the guest of my brother's brother-in-law, Gerald Balding. I am very beautiful but have no idea of this and I am a very shy teenager. Back home in England my mother is in a coma following a cata-strophic riding accident, and the memories of the lovely home that we lived in, filled with all the sweet furnishings of a happy childhood, are being slowly rubbed out forever. In the circus in America I saw a vision of the future, a happy place, cared for and loved, where chil-dren and animals played together in the sunshine and the work place was a huge candy striped tent, full of music.

This was my childhood. My dad is a film director and much younger than my mum. I have two older sisters, an older brother and a younger sister. First we lived in Oxford and then we lived in Wiltshire. Big houses, not much money, non-stop fun – friends, family, books, paintings – a threadbare, beauti-ful Bohemian life. That was what stopped when my mother's terrible tragedy hap-pened. A broken life, cracks that will run relentlessly into the future, tearing us all apart, the ground falling away as we try to walk forward, valleys and gullies of pain streaming between us as we desperately try to clasp hands and hearts.

Left: Me at Folly Farm. (James Waddell)

When you lose your mother you lose yourself. The distinct person that you are to your mother you are to no one else. So that person has to be quiet then, forever, because no one else but your mother will hear them.

When I came back from working in America at Circus Flora I went to New College at the University of Oxford to read English. I had by this point decided that I wanted to run my own circus. The situation at home became more desperate as my mother made no signs at all of recovery and I fell into a dark place. I took a razor to my blonde curls and dressed in heavy boys' clothes. I felt as if I broke everything that I came into contact with. I had no idea what to do, how to relate to people or who I was. After finishing my final exams I bought an old van from an auction and joined the first circus that came to town, which was, if nothing else, a job and a shaky step towards what felt like an insurmountable dream.

For the next few years I worked on many different circus shows. I can't say that crawling through the mud in the middle of the night rolling up rubber stable mats, my throat burning with the fumes of elephant pee, was exactly what I had in mind, but it gave me something to do – a track, a path – and that path nonetheless made sense to me. And in a world of remorseless hard living, mud, wheels, metal stakes, ropes and roads, there was nothing to break except myself.

These were my first experiences of circus: Circus Flora in America, where I fell in love; and then this other world, England, the mid 1990s – a hard and negative world, and a bad time for circus. My impressions then, in England, were that the shows were in decline and that morale amongst circus people was low, as the public turned against their art. The circus was letting go of its own history, overwhelmed by new mediums of entertainment – a word whose meaning was slipping away.

Above left: This is me carrying seating boards at Circus Flora. I loved this heavy manual work, and discovered that I was surprisingly strong. I was incredibly proud of this. (Giffords Circus collection)

Right: Circus Flora. (Giffords Circus collection)

I spent the winter of 1997 living in a caravan on a farm on the outskirts of Cheltenham. I had been working on circus shows in the UK for about five years. I sold tickets, ice cream, hot dogs and sparkly wands. I saw the boss's children walk around the front of the shows counting ice-cream cones to make sure that we weren't fiddling the change. I drove vans and lorries, and towed caravans in endless night convoys, swung sledge hammers, pulled out tent canvas and raked sawdust. I rode Arab horses and an elephant, Beverley, who I used to draw between shows. I wore a top hat and tails and introduced acts and then, while working for a French family circus touring the South Coast, I started to help with circus administration. I booked grounds, negotiated with farmers and lobbied the councils to try and get fairer treatment for the circus. I felt indignation on behalf of the resigned circus directors for the non-stop bullying levied at them from every sector – the local authorities, the public, the police – and also felt the profound demoralisation of shows attended by only twenty or thirty people. I did solo publicity parades around supermarket car parks to try and drum up business.

I learnt to make improvised showgirl costumes – I found out where you ordered the sequins and the spangles and the stretchy fabric. I frequented car-boot sales with circus girls, born and bred, and learnt to scout for glass jewellery and old swimwear. Caravan living and talk – gangs of homesick Hungarian mechanics, underpaid and overworked, longing for the rivers and sunshine of their homes, broken-handed, living on £6 a week. Highly trained clowns from the Eastern Bloc circus school, experienced in music, movement, acrobatics. Circus girls who between shows stitched their car-boot treasures into costumes, who

Above left: This is me riding an elephant in a show in Scotland. (Giffords Circus collection)

Above right: At Santus Circus box office. (Rick Stroud)

Right: These are my drawings of Beverley, the elephant I rode. (Nell Gifford)

mended their tights with tiny spider-web stitches and drank coffee laced with Tia Maria from smoked-glass tea sets. The non-stop struggle to survive – midnight raids, attacks from gypsies, the endless form-filling that could crush a soul whose core business is risking their own life to make people clap. I was at a point of learning a trade where for a moment you think you know it all and then you realise that actually you know nothing; that you are only at a starting point.

In 1998 I was offered a job as a groom on a circus in Germany, Circus Roncalli.

In Germany I realised that the UK was truly at the bottom end of the circus world. In Europe I discovered, to my total astonishment, a circus culture as highly designed and celebrated as a gorgeous Fabergé egg. Here was a circus culture prized by a public who poured daily by the thousand through its perfectly oiled, gilded turnstiles to feast on iced biscuits and champagne, and be thrilled by the cream of Europe's grand circus dynasties. Bougliones, Caroli, Gruss – families who danced on galloping horses and leapt through flaming hoops, clad in exquisite costumes designed in Vienna. Here there were golden wagons full of seamstresses pressing silk shirts and scarlet wool coats, uniformed front-of-house staff who spoke eight languages and wore white gloves, Commedia dell'Arte stained-glass windows along the front of the vast row of box office wagons. Here was a dynamic network of artistes, direc-tors, designers and choreographers, a whirl of Winter Gardens, the Moulin Rouge and circus festivals, each driving up the stand-ard of popular entertainment, leaving the

Above: My dad, Rick, took this picture of me and Toti just after we got engaged. (Rick Stroud)

Above left: Riding one of Yasmine's horses Porto. (Rick Stroud)

Above right: Me in the circus cafe wagon. (Rick Stroud)

empty seats of the English circuses completely in the dark.

I was so excited to go to Germany. But before I left, something happened. When a tall, curly-haired boy with a smudgy oily face smiles at you and drives you to see your sister in Yorkshire in a tractor, what do you do? You fall in love, of course. His name was Toti Gifford.

I did not want to leave Toti at all, but I wanted to go to Germany. I would be working with Yasmine Smart, the granddaughter of Billy Smart, and she was a world-famous circus equestrienne. So I went. Toti visited the circus every few weeks and there were many broken-hearted farewells at train stations. I cried in the rain at Düsseldorf train station as he was whisked away from me on the Eurostar, and cried with happiness when

I saw him four weeks later. We walked in the gardens of a nearby Schloss on our day off, and when the circus journeyed down into southern Germany in high midsummer, the heat in the tent hitting 40°C, we explored the castles, alleys and libraries of Heidelberg.

But mainly, that time was about the shows. We moved about once every two months, always to big cities. I was overwhelmed by Circus Roncalli: its immaculate veneer, its velvet halls, its embossed and engraved wagons, its miles of sparkling festoon lights, its perfect shimmering Art Deco design. It is a massive German circus that pulses with a kind of gold, red velvet shiny presence in the grand cities that it visits – it exhumes a frosty sugary smell, the sound of kitten heels dancing on wooden boards and the notes of a brass band, a violin player as

sweet as honey, visions of dappled horses under high municipal lime trees and dancing girls like soldiers with glittering eyes. I was a gauche 18-year-old again caught in the headlights of a circus show that seemed to encapsulate everything I wanted in life. This was the velvet-clad, rarefied world of the international circus community and I was star struck.

Francesco Caroli standing on a deep-ply red carpet in the dark and brilliant spot light of the ring, his blue Pierrot costume, a vintage heirloom from Paris, twinkling and sparkling as a thousand rhinestones refract the lights.

'Meine Herren, Meine Damen, Meine Kinder – das Spiel beginnt!'

In 1999 Toti and I returned to England, got married and immediately decided to start our own circus. We had no money, equipment or backing. We named our circus, in the old style, with the family name – Giffords Circus. Our garden shed was our office and we bought an ex-hire white tent from an advert in the local paper.

Married life has been circus life. This book is an account of the first ten years of Giffords Circus. Over this time we have entertained over 200,000 people. We have travelled the world in search of artistes, musicians and directors – Budapest, Bucharest, Moscow, Paris – we have watched thousands of hours of circus, rehearsals and training. We have lived and worked with Parisian musicians, Ossetian horsemen, Hungarian farmers, Romanian artisans, Ethiopian brothers, runaways and rebels. This is their story, and ours.

Above: Me and Toti outside our rented cottage. (Jacqui Harrison)

Right: Defining equestrienne. (Nell Gifford)

Giffords Circus group photograph, 2002.
(James Waddell)

MY FIRST CIRCUS

Toti and I started Giffords Circus in 2000. However, many years before that – back in the day, before Mum's accident and before I left home – my sister Clover and I created a circus birthday party for some friends of ours. We borrowed the village church marquee and decorated it with cut-out cardboard flowers, we did fancy dress and served a big tea. The curious thing about this is that the little girl, Maisie, whose party it was, who can be seen in old photographs from that day handing out the tray of cakes, has helped run our circus restaurant, and her mum, Penny Rose, is our circus fairy godmother.

Left: Maisie handing out the cakes. Clover and I made the flowers around the tent. (Penny Rose)

Right: The poster for the circus birthday party. (Nell Gifford)

CIRCUS

AFTER SOME DELIBERATION, CLOVER AND I DECIDED ON THE THEME OF CIRCUS FOR THE PARTY. WE'VE GOT OUR OWN SMALL BIG TOP, WHICH WE WILL DECORATE WITH CREPE, BALLOONS AND BIG COLOURFUL CUT-OUT FLOWERS. ALSO CUT-OUT ANIMALS, SUCH AS THE ELEPHANT IN THE PICTURE. IN THE WAY OF ANIMALS - THE REAL THING - WE ARE TALKING ABOUT A PONY AND CART, A MINIATURE SHETLAND, A PERM PERFORMING DOG CALLED RAGS AND POSSIBLY A TAME SHEEP. THE ENTERTAINMENTS CAN INCLUDE A CLOWN OR TWO, EGG AND SPOON RACE WITH REAL EGGS, EATING DOUGHNUTS OFF STRING — NO HANDS ALLOWED, DRESSING UP AND FACE-PAINTING, A SAWDUST LUCKY DIP AND OF COURSE SOME FAIR-GROUND MUSIC. WHAT ELSE DID WE THINK OF?... A BIG DRUM FOR ALL TO PLAY, AND DANGLING FROM THE TENT ROOF A POSITIVE GALAXY OF STARS.

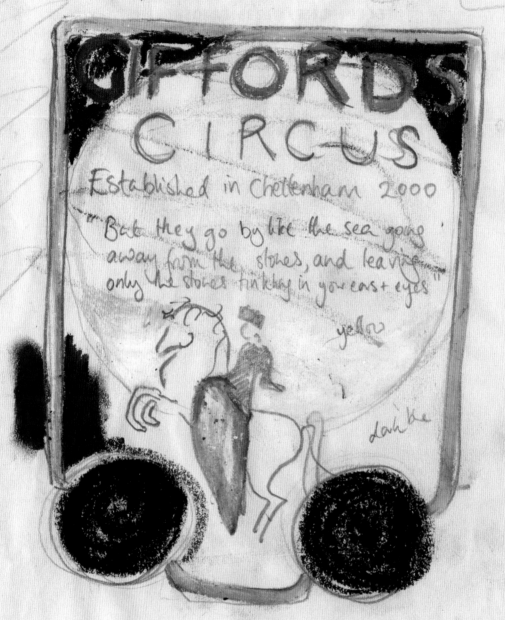

BUROUNN

GIFFORDS
CIRCUS
Established in Cheltenham 2000

"But they go by like the sea going
away from the stones, and leaving
only the stones tinkling in your ears + eyes"

yellow

dark blue

Presented by Toti and Nell Gifford
Established in in 2000 in Cheltenham.
2 0 0 0
The smallest show on earth.

THE RED DRESS

oon after Toti and I got married in 1999, we started the circus. I moved out of my caravan and into the little cottage that Toti rented. Toti plastered the shed in the garden and we used it as an office. The first few steps were tentative and controlled. We were suspending disbelief. Each new step felt like a step towards a kind of voluntary disaster. It was, I can say now, an utterly exhausting process.

We wondered what we should call our circus. We played around with some names – Carousel, Pegasus, The Circus of the Moon Globe – but all these names felt disconnected, as if we were trying to trick someone. Our aim was to start a circus that would be evocative of a village-green circus from your remembered childhood, or from a story book, or a dream – from a part of your mind where all these things get mixed up, the place where lost things hide, a place where pure image and sensation float on a fragile surface, beautiful yet ungraspable because as you reach towards them the image floats away in the ripples. Do you remember a white tent, twinkling fairy lights and a procession of dancing horses? Do you remember shadows of curtains and lights, and somebody beautiful in a little wagon like a bathing machine, like a gypsy? Were you them, or did you want to be them? Many times I have felt that the putting together of our circus is the search-

ing for a lost childhood – fragments, old toys, broken books, a fancy dress parade. Time and time again in the shows, strange characters and episodes from childhood have popped up in the show – Napoleon, The Weather Cockerel – as if summoned. I find this curious and deeply magical.

Still, we could not find the right name for the circus. Then I did what I find I have to do now when solving a creative problem, which is to think directly and clearly. I have to ask myself the question in simple terms.

Left: So we called it Giffords Circus. (Nell Gifford)

Right: I think my mum liked to dress me as a troubadour. (Rick Stroud)

What is this circus? What is it, truthfully? In its most simple explanation, what is it? And then the answer was there in front of us: it was our family circus. This circus was to be mine and Toti's show, a family show. So we called it Giffords Circus.

From the warmth of the little shed in the garden I set up a filing system. I bought one small ring-bind purple file and divided into sections – Acts, Rides, Horses, Costumes, Insurance. I showed this file to Toti, who said that it would be better to have a separate file per section. I remember feeling doubtful; it seemed extravagant – too many files. I am recounting this because this small tentative system has grown to the point where, ten years later, each of these sections now has its own building and its own team.

We did not have a fixed idea as to when the circus should actually start, and so when I got a request from Hay-on-Wye Literary Festival to do a talk as part of the 2000 festival, we suggested to them that they should book our circus, Giffords Circus. No actual material circus existed then, only the name, an idea, a wish – a foresight maybe. I described the circus to the director: 'There will be showgirls and a dancing horse and a motorbike and a raucous atmosphere, lit by gaslight.' What promises! The director liked the sound of the show, and so we agreed a fee and the booking was made. This was in October 1999 and the festival was May 2000. We had a deadline.

That Hay-on-Wye booking was really the start. We started work on the physical structure of the circus. We had learnt from the time spent on Circus Roncalli that the exterior of the circus – the tent, the wagons and the landscape – was as much a part of the circus as the show, and that to build quality into the circus architecture was crucial. We did not really write a business plan, or find funding partners, we just started building wagons, hand to mouth, picking

Above: Our first wagon and our home. (Vladimir Eatwell)

Above left: Venetia. (Giffords Circus collection)

Above right: This is the letter to the director of the festival – our first booking. (Giffords Circus collection)

up enthusiasts as we went. We wanted the circus to feel like a vintage showpiece – old timber showman's wagons, vintage lorries, vintage fairground rides. We also needed a tent, a circus ring and seats. We planned to build a wagon for us to live in, and a wagon with bunk rooms for the performers, a shower wagon and wardrobe, and an office wagon. We were starting completely and totally from scratch – neither Toti nor I had any family who owned circus companies, so there was no handing down of old equipment, or advice, or anything. No, instead, nail by nail, stitch by stitch, we were going to build the whole thing from nothing. The task was huge although, looking back, I am sure we did not realise just how huge, or at what cost, in terms of our personal life. The terrible price that art extracts from life.

Toti found the shell of an old showman's wagon in a hedge. He dragged it out of the hedge and down to the yard. At that time Toti kept his machinery in an agricultural yard near Cheltenham which was owned by his grandfather, a kind erudite farmer called David Smith, a true countryman. David's yard would give us the space to build a circus, and for some time, a place to live. It was a complete wreck and had no floor or ceiling.

We started to mend the wagon, but the work was very slow and money was tight. Toti landscaped. I finished a book. To bring in some extra cash I joined a gang of travellers and Eastern European students, picking apples on a nearby fruit farm. Clambering around in the boughs of the plum trees with views out over the Welsh borders, the sound of the pickers' radios all blaring out BBC Radio 4, it was a relatively carefree autumn. It all seemed, at that point, quite simple. The going appeared flat and easy, and we strode forward with happy steps.

While living at the cottage we went to a steam rally to look at the wagons and rides, and I remember standing on the steps of a wagon looking at its beautifully restored interior, all cut-glass and polished hardwood. We said to the owner that we had just bought an old run-down wagon and she sucked her teeth and said that they cost a fortune to restore. I asked how much and she said twenty grand. Twenty grand! We barely had a few hundred pounds between us. We had only just started, and right at that moment, in the bright autumn sunlight, it seemed impossible. Toti said not to worry, that it was an exaggeration.

In that autumn of 1999 we bought a 1910 hand-cranked children's chairoplane roundabout and a small white tent from the *Trade It* newspaper. We also started to spend more time with the fruit pickers. There was Ben – a quiet, good-looking Australian man with long dreadlocks – his wife Julia and their baby. He was a typical New Age traveller – austere and corrective, someone who, through a mixture of rebelliousness and distaste for the consumer world, had withdrawn into a ramshackle homemade world of benders, buses and horse-drawn vehicles to live a more frugal existence; ecowarriors. They busked, worked on farms and sold cups of tea at festivals. They recycled, cooked on fires and washed in buckets of water. Ben and Julia lived this lifestyle to the full, carving out a cosy intricate interior in the horse box in which they lived with their baby – it was a grotto of drapes and candles and little pictures, a barn owl perched in the corner, a stove glowing brightly. There was little Ali, who played the penny whistle and kept fastidious accounts; Taffy, a depressed Welshman; John, a long-haired Prospero, and his girlfriend who was said to descend from Lady Jane Grey and was two hundredth in line to the throne; Luke, a dark-eyed shaven-headed mechanic who was between prison spells; and Jan, an old woman who lived in a British Telecoms van in which there was a fully functioning Rayburn. They were a mixture of runaways,

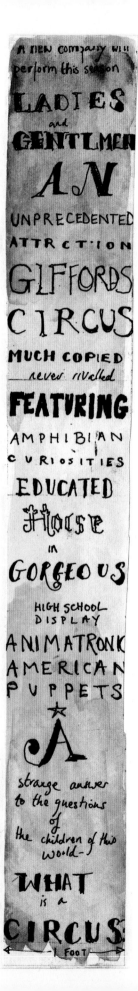

Left: Early artwork.
(Nell Gifford)

convicts and people who had consciously absconded from the modern world. But they were also people whose illnesses and phobias meant that they just could not exist surrounded by the pace of the modern world and had, therefore, retreated to the hedgerows for salvation and survival. There was however one characteristic they all shared – they loved to party.

We drank with them in the White Hart in Winchcombe and afterwards went back to the fruit pickers' field where we sat around the fire, drank cider, watched sparks flying and dogs circling, and talked about freedom and beauty and truth. I felt very happy. One night we stayed in an old four-poster bed set up outside under the stars and ink-coloured sky.

Ben and Julia came to work with us at David's yard. Ben turned out to be a trained painter and signwriter. Luke also joined us, as a mechanic. I caught up with an old friend from school, Venetia, and she too gamely came to join us and immersed her-self in our world.

Venetia had no experience in carpentry but she understood very well the artistic aspirations of the show and this was a life-line, for during those winter months as things seemed to close in around us, it was hard to remember what the idea was in the first place. Now, thirteen years later, the show has a modest art department helping to drive and define ideas. I understand now that the creation phase, which is what that period of time basically was, is fragile and has to be recorded, written down, endlessly defined and documented. The show has to be researched, developed and articulated. But during those early days I had no real idea of this, and felt constantly ridiculous. Voices in my head were saying that it was all folly. I ignore them now, those voices, and I am starting to understand that this instinct for creating something is actually a talent and of value. Venetia helped me by being there as someone to talk to, to have ideas with, to be excited with; as someone to suggest that, at the end of all this, there might be something very beautiful, if we just kept trying, if we dared.

The fruit-picking season ended. We were putting all the money and time that we had into the project. Unable to pay the rent for the cottage, we had to leave. That was when the pressure started. We were homeless. After a hasty packing-up of stuff, we piled everything into our car. David, somewhat bemused in his spectacles and well-worn Barbour coat, good-naturedly agreed that we could live in the yard for a while. There was no option but to move into the half-repaired wagon in the yard. I remember the day we finally left the cottage. The sun was setting. It was a bright golden sunset, weirdly bright, and the sky was very dark. There was a carved wooden hare in the garden. The sun lit the wooden hare and it turned to the colour of blood. We left the blood hare there, in the garden, silent and still against the iron sky.

We sat around the fire, drank cider, watched sparks flying and dogs circling, and talked about freedom and beauty and truth.

The wagon was not finished when we moved out of the cottage, so for a while we slept on floors and the spare room of a pub. Every day was spent at the yard or on building sites with Toti, walling and stone picking. Life fell into a routine of sanding, de-nailing old piles of timber, sawing, drilling and painting. It seemed to rain constantly. Our crude workshop, hastily put up by Toti in the year, was lit by one strip light. Every day we built wagons. We were constantly filthy and very tired. Then we ran out of money. Toti sold his machines. We sold our car. Toti's sister sent us £50 in the post for food.

This desperate time took its toll on the team. Venetia and I were too tired for friendship. We all probably drank too much – every evening, exhausted and freezing, we would fall into the Hungry Horse pub over the road, wash our hands in the sinks, eat cheap food and drink beer until we were asleep, often in the pub. The amicable Scottish landlord, Gareth, became our friend. He stopped charging us for food. That pub was as good as home for us that winter. Soaking wet concrete, wet breeze-block walls, the sound of traffic on the road, and every day the wolf howling at the door. Money was not just tight, it had run out completely – we sold everything, we borrowed, we were in negative equity.

We ran ourselves into debts of over £100,000 and at times had such bad rows that it seemed that the sky had fallen in over our heads. We did not have time for family or friends or fun. We lost touch with people and we often felt completely alone. We felt very stupid and humiliated. We wanted to be back in the cottage starting a family and saving. We avoided debt collectors and lived off nothing. We were completely stubborn and sustained only by a shared dream, one that twinkled on a far-off village green like a mirage.

May 2000 was getting closer and we had no show and no wagons finished. We had no money to finish the wagons, which did not even have wheels.

Sometime in the depths of that winter, Gerald Balding – the long-haired, bearded, noisy wild brother of my brother's wife – roared into town on his brightly coloured motorbike with a backpack full of glue and wire, bits of fabric and puppet limbs. It was Gerald who had first invited me to join the circus in America, Circus Flora – it was owned by his uncle. Then, living back

Right: The first poster, drawn by Venetia. (Venetia Nathan)

in England, Gerald decided to throw his lot in with ours and join Giffords Circus. By then the team were all engrossed in wagon building. It was Gerald who asked the very relevant question as to what was actually going to be in the circus show. I can say now that he was the first person who asked me this question, and he then sat down with me to work through the answer. It is a very important question indeed, and it is a question that, as long as you are producing shows, will not go away.

'Let us just for a moment create one little bubble of magic in that tent,' he would eulogise, his enthusiasm breathing energy into our tired gang. He, Venetia and I started to think through the show itself. I wanted a troupe of dancers to segue between the acts. Gerald had his motorbike and a skeleton puppet. I had my horse, a black-and-white filly that was a wedding present from my aunt, which I kept at some stables up the road from the yard.

Around this time, Venetia and I went to visit Jan, the old lady who lived in the electric BT van. We went to give her something, or to have a cup of tea – I can't remember. But I do remember the cold wet grass of the verge where she was parked, and her dirty cracked hands showing us an old tin toffee box. She wanted us to choose a stone each from the box. She prised the lid open and there it was, on the inside of the lid – the red dress. It was a beautiful drawing of a girl who seemed to be flying past in a red skirt made of red snakes, adorned with a necklace of red feathers. Venetia and I both instantly recognised it as being somehow ours, as if it was just there to be discovered – it was a Giffords Circus costume. Many times I have this sensation as I research shows, that I am searching and searching for some kind of lost fragment. So the act of making the show becomes a kind of reassembling of something I have lost.

Above: The girl in the red dress. (Venetia Nathan)

Venetia traced and painted the girl in the red dress. We decided we would make three of them, for our three dancers.

Gerald, Venetia and I organised an audition at The Playhouse Theatre in Cheltenham. The jury on the day consisted of: me, Gerald, Venetia and two circus friends of mine, Julie and Michelle Fossett. Julie and Michelle are seventh- and eighth-generation circus girls, mother and daughter. Born and brought up on the road; you name it, these girls had done it – spun candy floss, walked wires, swung on trapezes, ridden elephants, welded, driven all night. They appeared as they always do – an immaculate turn-out of floor-length zebra-print coats, fur collars, false eyelashes, snake-skin high-heel studded boots, nail varnish and hair pieces, all delivered in a cloud of heavy perfume.

The five of us sat in the seats of the theatre and waited for the dancers to arrive. In the end just three girls arrived from the hundreds of CVs I had been sent. We hired all three of them. A sturdy girl from Birmingham also appeared and showed us her contortion routine. It was good; it won the approval of the Fossetts. As did Dorien, a polite gentleman juggler from Cheltenham. In the excitement, Nicky the contortionist left. I panicked that we had lost her so quickly called her mobile and offered her the job. She accepted. It was my first experience of the endless task of finding and chasing artistes.

We were building our first little company of performers. I made contact through the festival circuit with a brilliant man who could walk on a rope and play the violin at the same time; he could also walk on stilts and do handstands. He was called Kwabana Lindsay, lived in a blue truck and was a solitary, shy man who came alive when he painted his face white, pulled on his starry shirt and danced on a rope while playing a violin. I tracked down Joe, an old

friend from Oxford who played the guitar, and he brought his beautiful voice and a drummer called Peter Sen.

Joe and Peter arrived at our agricultural yard on a windy early spring day. Joe had a can of beer in his hand and a stack of old children's LPs under his arm, which were to make up some of the soundtrack, including vintage recordings of 'She'll be Coming Round the Mountain'. Pete wore a white flowing highwayman's shirt; his hair was long and black, and tumbled about his shoulders in glossy optimistic curls. He was half-Indian, half-English, and his manner was serious and shy.

I was starting to realise that shy people make great performers. The bunk wagon was just about finished so Peter and Joe moved in with us, taking a tiny room with bunk beds – the other rooms were for the three dancers, the contortionist Nicky and Dorien the juggler.

These people were our first company.

The spring was coming and in some ways we had found a new momentum as we staggered out of winter. I cannot remember exactly how we pieced it together. I remem-

Above: Clover and Peter Sen on the steps of the bunk wagon. (Giffords Circus collection)

ber a visit to London with Venetia to find red fabric for the red dresses – it was the opening up of a new world of fabric markets, button suppliers, Berwick Street, Goldhawk Road, the Indian shops in Southhall, and the endless variations of red: silks, satins, two-way stretch velvets. Manifesting visions. I remember endless trips to a paint shop in Gloucester, and the frustration of trying to find the exact shade of burgundy that we had in mind. Burgundy, cream, pale blue – our colours, floating in front of us. I remember the endless sanding and undercoating, and I remember wishing spring would stand still so that we would

have more time: more time to make everything ready; more time before we set off on the road.

The miracle of a freshly painted wagon appearing from the rusty old shed was a sign that we could do it. I would love to look back and say that all this was well organised and that the leadership that Toti and I gave to this committed, hardworking gang was flawless, but I know it wasn't. It was run on momentum and passion, by fire-fighting problems as they came up, by the sound of the word 'circus'. Yes, just that word; I am sure it was to do with that – circus, circus, circus. In our dusty paint-

spattered clothes, our old cars, our tireless alcohol-fuelled enthusiasm, our embracing of each other's eccentricities, in the way we made each other laugh from time to time, in our fascination for bringing to life picture books rescued from the bottom of a forgotten charity shop library, with our old records, our musical instruments, our new wagons, our pony that could bow and our painted bikes, dancing puppets, waxed moustaches and folk songs learnt by rote like nursery rhymes for a grown-up broken heart, we were living the dream.

The Hay-on-Wye date loomed closer. Gareth, the landlord of the pub opposite who was by now almost ready to come on the road with us he was so involved in the project, kindly offered his pub field as an opening ground. We would then stop in Ross-on-Wye, before heading to Hay for the festival. It is hard to imagine the volume of stuff that you need when you take a circus on the road – torches, cable

ties, rope, string, scissors, stakes, sledge hammers, canvas, poles, clips and shackles of all sizes, shavings, rakes, shovels, wheel barrows, muck carts, washing-up liquid, bowls, towels, duvets, sponges, coal, coal tongs, boots, coats, electric fans, electric heaters, umbrellas, dustbins, clogs, riding shoes, ballet shoes, tap shoes, trainers, blankets, television sets, stocked make-up bags, tights, fishnets, wigs, cotton wool, boxes, flight cases, hundreds of coat hangers, tent walls, linings, metres of velvet curtain, masks, shoe-cleaning-kits … it takes us six weeks now to pack for a tour and six weeks to unpack.

But in those early days we simply got up and left. So much was left to chance, and there were so many essential tools of mobile organisation that we simply could not afford. We did not have any lorries. An old friend of Toti's, Miles, who ran a one-man removal business, very gamely offered us his van and his time, although

Above: The dancers in the red dress costume. (Giffords Circus collection)

we had to fit in – understandably – around house moves. We did have a very old dumper truck, and when the time came to cross the road from our yard to the pub, Toti simply hitched the dumper truck to the wagons, which still did not have wheels, and dragged them, screeching, down the road. A couple of the farmer workers stopped their tractors and stared in amazement. David gave us a great cheer. Gareth came out of the pub and gamely held up the traffic for us. We must have looked completely mad. Young, wild-haired, sparks flying, broke, and fixated on what seemed to be an impossible dream.

Toti started to put the tent up with Gerald, Pete, Joe and a new helper called Ian Rumbelow, a cheerful, handsome painter and decorator who was dating David's daughter. Our three dancers sat on a grassy bank watching, and probably wondering just what kind of contract they had signed up for. The tent went up very slowly. The dancers

practised their routines in the car parks – luckily one of the girls could choreograph.

On the day before opening we still did not have any seats or a ring fence. We borrowed plastic chairs from a village hall and, in a stroke of luck, some circus people who lived in Chipping Norton who had stopped touring offered to lend us their old ring fence.

I look back at the photographs now and I can see an extraordinarily bare tent, two musicians, a contortionist in a red catsuit and some dancers dressed as clowns, me in an old riding suit on a horse and Toti looking wild and thin with oily hands.

Perhaps it was blind optimism that kept us going. Certainly we set the ticket prices very high for the first show – we decided to match West End prices. I think that the opening night tickets were about £50 each, which the audience – made up entirely of supporting friends and family, led by one of my mother's oldest friends Caroline Mann – obligingly paid.

Above: Kwabana Lindsay on the steps of the box office. (Giffords Circus collection)

Right: Kwabana on the rope. (David Waddell)

The sun shone on that opening evening, which was a blessing. Gareth put on his best shirt and handed around drinks. The dancers wore exquisite front-of-house costumes made for us by David's wife. The chairoplane roundabout turned, cranked (backwards, it has to be admitted) by Prospero John from the fruit fields.

The audience was enthusiastic. The dancers danced in their new red costumes; the motorbike roared. My cousin James came to help Toti, and he and Toti did some impromptu comedy as they were moving the props in and out. Joe swigged his beer and sang his heart out and Pete hit his drum kit like a pro, oiled black locks bouncing. 'I would be a fisherman, with light in my eyes, and you in my arms, I will be a fisherman!'

A friend of Toti's, an artist and inventor called Dan Chadwick, came on that opening night – he said that the girls in the red dresses and the 'Fisherman's Blues' together made him cry. Someone else said that we were like Edwardian children playing at circus. These scraps of feedback were like jewels – a sign that something was working.

Unfortunately, the revenue quickly dried up and we found ourselves with a show that was not selling any tickets and the wages of the company still to pay. After one weekend we left the Hungry Horse pub at Severn Springs for Hay-on-Wye, Gareth waving tearfully from the pub doorway.

Those opening shows got us to Ross-on-Wye, where we did little or no business at all. Joe knew the landlady of one of the pubs in town and, grabbing a handful of unsold tickets, set off for the bar. He reappeared at the circus having sold not a single ticket. 'They are all lazy in there and they

Above: First show. Supermodel Iris Palmer on the curtain, an audience of friends. (Giffords Circus collection)

Right: Gerald and Toti. I took this picture and love it. (Nell Gifford)

don't want to come. They just want to sit at the bar and drink,' he said with disgust. 'It's terrible.' This was funny coming from Joe, as his life was pretty much one long sit at a pub bar, but suddenly it seemed we were all on the other side of things somehow.

We paraded around town in our costumes. I rode my horse, Eclipse, the dancers dressed in their cancan dresses handed out hastily photocopied fliers, and Pete and Joe banged drums and sang, but the people of Ross-on-Wye could not have been less interested. We then tried to give away some tickets. Toti found a group of Brownies in the park on an outing and gave them all free tickets; that was one of the only shows in Ross-on-Wye that we did not have to cancel. An audience that has come in for free is better than no audience at all.

Show after show was cancelled. I remember standing at the top of the steps of my wagon talking to Gerald and Venetia, telling them that we would have to cancel one of the shows. Gerald looked so smart in his waxed moustache and top hat and Venetia beautiful in a green dress, show-ready. They looked disappointed and perplexed. It was then that I started to realise how profoundly the house sizes would affect morale, and that the audience numbers were my responsibility. I was a show producer, and at that moment not a remotely successful one.

By the end of the week at Ross we were quite literally penniless, save a few hundred pounds that Toti had with his (now worried-looking) accountant in Ross-on-Wye. The accountant made this small reserve available and that, together with the last of the money that had come in on those opening nights and some change from programme sales, meant that we were somehow able to pay the wages and fill the tanks to get to Hay-on-Wye.

It was in the middle of the night, on the winding road to Hay, that the vehicles started to break down; oil and water on dark tarmac, hazard lights. The dancers

Above: Toti and me with Loulee and Lydia, two of Toti's four sisters. (Rick Stroud)

displayed blank expressions, longing for rest. Ben and Toti, lightheaded from lack of sleep, sweat pouring down their faces, started dragging the wagons into town one by one with the last remaining running vehicle, an old Land Rover. The last load was a Land Rover hitched to a caravan and that caravan onto another Land Rover, behind which was a trailer attached to which was our heavy hired generator. They dragged this rusty cavalcade into town; relentless, illegal and unstoppable.

By the time we arrived in Hay, Toti and I had no money whatsoever: no coppers, nothing. We managed to get our troupe in place with their wagon, Lindsay's bus and Gerald's caravan, and then we just collapsed into the darkness of our wagon. We were parked near to the cattle market. When we woke up it was market day and the wagons were surrounded by cattle and Welsh farmers. We were so hungry. We had a day to wait before we could get onto the cattle market and put the tent up. I went down to the festival site to see if they had sold any tickets and if I could get some money for food. To my amazement, Giffords Circus was the most popular event of the festival after Bob Geldof, and had completely sold out.

The following six shows were totally packed out. Packed. The joy, the absolute joy of a packed show: packed, sweaty, breathless, sexy, bawdy, noisy. Joe thrashed out the Irish folk music, the girls danced and Kwabana bounced on his rope, the violin singing at a million miles an hour, the tent jumping and creaking with the rope. High on success, exhaustion and exhilaration, our little company did not stop partying for the entire festival.

Hay-on-Wye took us to a media audience. It gave us a sign that Giffords Circus could work – would work. We returned to the yard in a state of disarray; confused, excited, broke. There seemed to be only one option: plan another tour.

3

THE WHITE DRESS
OUR COMPANY GROWS

The two years following our breakneck debut in Hay-on-Wye's cattle market are difficult to remember in detail. We were on a very steep learning curve as we fought to keep the circus solvent and touring. We learnt and built systems, experimenting and backtracking. We learnt that the people of Ross-on-Wye did not want, under any circumstances, to turn out to see Giffords Circus, even when we had given them free tickets. We continued to play at Hay Literary Festival and we continued to be seen there by a media audience. This aided our profile in the early days and helped us to define who we were.

We learnt to interact with a community as a circus company – Toti making friends with the Welsh sheep dealers and the bustling auctioneers, the local mechanics and builders. The publicans were sometimes suspicious, sometimes embracing, a sign of slow acceptance from the locals. Over time I think we became known as a kind of travelling party, as the late-night lock-ins increased in length and frequency. At Hay-on-Wye we were never really formally invited to the exclusive media parties but we took it upon on ourselves to gatecrash them all, to the point where we almost felt that this was our job, as if it would be almost rude not to. It was unbelievably good fun. Late nights, dancing, drinking. Hay Literary Festival is a riotously great

Left: The white dress hanging in the back tent. Toti made a decision early on that all spaces, public and private, should be lit by chandeliers. (James Waddell)

event – thousands of people, lots of parties, lots of ideas – they have nailed how to make a festival transcendentally exciting, as if anything might happen. Smuggling Cossack riders into the *Guardian* party, past the uptight London PR girl and security, the boys silent, smiling and handsome in their best suits, finding out some names on the guest list and pretending that these hard-living wild men from the Caucasus were guest authors, and getting away with it – heady and hilarious times.

We took the circus to my old village of Minety where we played on Toti's aunt's front field. It was wonderful to have the support of old friends. Sidney Bailey, the local huntsman who was Clover's and my childhood hero, smiling and economical with words, brought his hounds to see the circus. Past and present collided. Dominic Waldron, who had come on so many cart rides with me as a grubby-faced blonde-haired little boy, joined the circus.

We had to find more grounds so Toti and I visited our old friend Mark Palmer, who had spent many summers travelling the villages greens in his brightly coloured wagon. Sitting in his green-painted kitchen, the light shining through dusty glass and the apple trees beyond, he wrote out some suggestions on the back of an envelope: Minchinhampton; Frampton-on-Severn.

This is still the backbone of the tour to this day. Over the years we have developed

a relationship with these places and with the people who run them – our experience of rural England is that it is often run by local people in the most balanced and egalitarian way possible. For example, in Minchinhampton, which is National Trust common land, the Committee of Commoners – a group of about fifty local people – put an extraordinary amount of work into the administration of the common to make sure that the locals, dog walkers, stockmen with grazing rights, the circus, retired people and the local teenagers are all taken into consideration.

The people of Minchinhampton and the surrounding Stroud valleys proved themselves to have an insatiable appetite for circus. It was as if we could not put on enough shows. They kept appearing; by car, on foot, on horses. For the first time we could confidently schedule as many shows as we wanted, knowing that they would be full. We are grateful to the people of the Stroud valleys; I think that the start of the circus would have been much harder without them. A full tent means money coming in, and furthermore it gives us energy. It forces the show to its full potential. It creates excitement in the tent and this raises the stakes for the audience and for the performers. We made friends with the local vicar, Michael Irving, because he used to wander across the green and come and have tea with us after the morning service. Ten years later he christened our twins in Gloucester Cathedral. We met our bank manager on that common – I was walking the dogs, he was biking across the tufty cattle-grazed grass towards the circus. He stopped to say hello and introduced himself. We started talking about the circus. He said he was a local bank manager and would be interested to meet us in Cirencester to discuss the business, which we did. He now manages the circus accounts, and is a trusted friend.

Above: Giffords Circus – ahead of its time. When I look at this photograph I realise that we were doing burlesque before burlesque came to England. It is now a fashionable theatrical sub-culture in London. (James Waddell)

GIFFORDS CIRCUS

TRAVEL BACK IN TIME TO THE WORLD OF A 1930's CIRCUS, TOURING THIS SUMMER IN THE COTSWOLDS

Right: Our first flier. (Giffords Circus collection)

We also learnt to sharpen up our publicity material. We designed a colourful flier with lots of photographs and detailed copy on it, written by me, describing Toti's and my life history and background – a near-enough mini essay of what Giffords Circus was all about.

The show rocked on. Graham rode his bike, I rode my horse and Toti drove the lorries. Kwabana Lindsay leapt and bounced on his rope playing the violin and juggling fire. Lost moments – I remember a fire-lit scene in the tent with sparkly showgirl costumes and Kwabana topless. The two girls were dripping in velvet and diamante on Minchinhampton Common, swinging on an outdoor trapeze rig they had set up. There is little documentation of some of these early moments – we did not realise then how important it was to photograph and film everything.

I fell in love with a little drawing I found in a book of make-your-own soft toys. It was a diagram of a circus ballerina on horseback.

Image and skill – this is the essence of circus production. I had the image but by no means had the skill. I did not know anyone who could do ballet standing on a horse. I did not know any ballerinas, and I did not even know anyone who could stand up on a horse. I had heard about the big Eastern European 'riding' (as this type of circus horsemanship is known) troupes but I had no idea how to find them or how to work with them if I did find them. The questions seemed complex – would they ride their own horses? Would we provide them? The size of our ring by normal circus standards is quite small – 30 feet across as opposed to 42 feet – would it be necessary to have a bigger ring in order to encompass this sort of act? This would have meant a bigger tent and investment beyond our reach.

Left: Helen and Sheena on their outdoor trapeze rig. (James Waddell)

Above: The ballerina on horseback I found in a book. (Giffords Circus collection)

The more I looked it into the idea, the more ballerinas I saw – in old circus engravings, posters, woodcuts and photographs. It was often a skill of the families of old circus proprieters but it had been phased out in this country almost altogether.

Then I saw an article in a local newspaper about the Windrush Vaulting Club. There were photographs of children and young people being trained to jump up on a horse as it cantered in a slow circle. Toti and I found out where their training sessions were held, which turned out to be a huge indoor ménage usually used for indoor carriage driving near Stow-on-the-Wold. I didn't dare to believe that the ballerina on horseback might be living in Stow-on-

the-Wold, just 10 miles from our yard. I remember this moment exactly – arriving at the vast school, lit by strip lights, surrounded by huge indoor mirrors. There she was in the mirror, the ballerina on horseback, standing with perfect balance on a huge grey horse that cantered in an effortless circle. The figure was bright against the dark glass of the mirror.

Rebecca Townsend and her mother ran the little club together. As a sport, equestrian vaulting is hugely popular on the continent and so the continental teams have good resources – specially trained horses, indoor

training spaces and a network of coaches. In England it is much more of a minority sport. Each week, Rebecca and her mother would box their two horses to the indoor arena. Here, Rebecca would lunge the horses (control them from the ground using a long lead rope and a long whip to prompt and guide, providing a backup for the voice) as they taught children from 7 years of age upwards. That day we watched as Rebecca's mother patiently explained to the shiny-eyed children how to run towards the horse in a rhythm that matched the horses canter, run alongside the horse and then reach up and grasp the handles at the top of the roller, and with one beautiful balletic movement swing upwards and across onto the back of the moving horse.

The horses rocked in their perfectly cadenced canters, the children stretched and pulled and swung onto the backs of the horses, the older children going two or even three up and forming balanced classical pyramids. To know that feeling, to sit on a horse as it moves at a canter, trusting you perfectly, the horse expecting soft

movement and kind words, giving in return a rocking, even gallop, neck arched, feet thudding and lifting on a soft surface – that is truly an adventure to fire a child's spirit – a perfect sport. At the end of each session the children would gather around the horse, patting it and rubbing its back where the roller and girth had been. Small hands grimy with horse dust, faces joyful – it was a deeply familiar connection, an English world where the pony is childhood.

I fell in love with this little club. They were so expert – Rebecca had represented the UK many times in equestrian vaulting and was seven times National Champion – but she and her mother avoided a toxic over-competitive attitude that some horse-world parents have, and instead took a genuine delight in the children and horses going well together. The welfare of the horse was paramount for Rebecca and her mother, and they taught the children to show the horse total kindness and consideration.

So we hung about the equestrian centre in Stow-on-the-Wold and we made friends with the red-headed, outspoken Rebecca

Above left and right: Rebecca Townsend training at the Windrush Vaulting Club. (Giffords Circus collection; James Waddell)

Right: A drawing towards the white dress. (Nell Gifford)

Rebecca

jump thro'
hoop?

backwards
somersault?

Dance
opposite
male
dancer.

love story

contemporary
music

long sleeves
e tailored

feater
trim

Nell Gifford
August 2003.

Townsend. The Cotswolds are known for their jet-set locals, and to some extent that is the case, but there is also an older and more rural community still at work. The big investors, the glitz people, help drive the tourist trade and this in turn provides jobs. It seems to me that many of the people who work in this economy come from an older Gloucestershire world – butchers, horse dealers, publicans, race horse trainers, gardeners. I feel lucky to live somewhere where there is so much work, where there is an inflow of interested visitors who will spend money on drinks, plants, shows and food. Rebecca comes from an old Cotswold farming family. She has thirteen uncles, who are all farmers. She told me they are so tight knit that one of the brothers who moved to the next-door market town, roughly 7 miles away, was deemed to have 'moved away'. Economic pressures and shifts in the agricultural economy mean that the farm Rebecca grew up on has an uncertain future, and so Rebecca, with her vaulting horses and training in ballet and gymnastics alongside her tough farm-girl resourcefulness, represents a very real agricultural diversification.

As we slowly made friends she accepted an offer to come and work on the show with us. The problem was that we did not have a horse suitable for this work. A vaulting horse (a ring or riding horse as it is known in the circus) needs to be trained to accept somebody moving about and standing on its back. It needs to work independently of the rider in a balanced, even gait, and respond immediately to voice commands such as 'Stand!', 'Walk on' or 'Trot on'. This training process takes a long time and cannot be rushed or you risk producing a horse that is nervous or inconsistent.

Rebecca, Toti and I met up in a little pub somewhere between Chipping Norton and Stow, Christmas lights festooned around us and festive songs playing, in order to try and thrash out a plan for the following season.

We were very unsure as to how a horse would work in our little ring. The public are very close-up and the ring is small. Rebecca's own horses were tall, and besides, they were the club horses so not available. Then we thought of Oliver Garrard. Oliver is an old friend of ours who lives in the Welsh borders and is a true horseman. He worked with Aborigines in Australia for several years. A semi-hermitic loner, he was at that time living in a caravan pulled by a black-and-white horse. I knew that he also had an old grey mare called Gee that walked behind the caravan. I remembered her being very large but not tall, and very quiet. I wondered whether she might work for the circus and whether Oliver would agree to lend her to us for the season. I called him and he agreed that we could bring Rebecca up to Shropshire to meet him and look at the mare.

It was a typical Oliver outing. We met in a pub near the wild heathland of Shropshire called the Long Mynd, which is part of the Shropshire Hills Area of Outstanding Natural Beauty. He had the grey mare with him, and the black-and-white wagon horse, who were both tied up outside the pub. It was January, an oddly mild day, overcast and still. We went inside and sat in the pub, the coal fire blazing. Oliver has this look about him as if he is always half-asleep. He shook hands with Rebecca as Toti bought a round of drinks. I can remember urgently wanting to talk to him about Gee; to see if she was available, if he would consider loaning her to us and if he thought she would walk about the circus ring at an even pace. But a horse deal is a horse deal, even with friends, and even when no money is going to change hands, it has to be done at the proper pace.

After the drinks we went outside to look at the horses. Oliver handed the grey mare to Rebecca.

Left: A mutual love affair – we loved Rebecca and Rebecca loved the circus. (James Waddell)

'Here, you two go up on Gee. Tots, you and me will go on Ivor.'

I clambered up onto Gee, who was wearing just a simple bridle, and then Rebecca vaulted neatly up behind me. Oliver looked at me and smiled. He and Toti then got up on Ivor, and the four of us, upon our two stocky cart horses, rode for the rest of the day across the Long Mynd, through deep valleys and across streams, emerging onto tracks, slipping and sliding off. The horses were alert and calm; everyone pleased to be amongst so much happiness and fresh air. Believe me, circus work is often long hours in office spaces banging away at computers. It is budgets and schedules; contracts, procedure and process. It is legalities, conflict resolution, bureaucracy, staff politics and appraisals. But just sometimes it is this – adventure and joy, and laughing for the whole day.

Oliver agreed to lend us Gee, and we made the white ballerina dress from the book. It fitted Rebecca like a glove.

Gee looked like a circus horse, and proved to be completely relaxed in the tent and in front of an audience. Our old friend Rob Mann led her around the ring while Rebecca somersaulted and danced on top of her. The picture was made – a real-life ballerina on a horse, sprung straight from a picture book.

The following year we bought a young Highland pony called Ronan. Rebecca trained him from scratch and he became her horse for the following two seasons. She subsequently bought him from us, and to this day he works with her, performing all over the country.

The ballerina on the horse was a potent image. James Waddell took a shot of Rebecca lying down on Gee as if asleep. We styled it with straw bales and starry fabric. It was a new way of seeing ourselves, and a step forward in this long process of defining who we were. I love that photograph – the quiet, pretty horse, the strange inside/

Above left: Farming stock – Rebecca backstage with Oleg, our Russian strongman. (James Waddell)

Above right: The white dress. (ArtScience)

outside quality of the set, Rebecca apparently lying fast asleep on top of the horse.

Rebecca, Toti and I had a ball. We made friends with Rebecca's boyfriend, a farrier called Duncan, and when Giffords Circus was used as the location for a fashion video, starring – yes – Rebecca and Ronan, and myself and Eclipse, we found ourselves sitting in the deep seats of the BAFTA screening rooms in Piccadilly, watching our own names up on the screen. We hit the town hard after that, toasting and drinking our fabulousness, as pay-off for those long winter months of mucking out and training in the dark. Heady times. Rebecca in the white dress was photographed for *Elle* and Italian *Vogue*. You can have ideas and designs your whole life but there may just be one or two key things that really work, and I think the white dress was one of mine. Add to that someone you really make friends with, and life and work collide joyfully.

The thirteen uncles, contrary to expectations, did come and see the show. It was the height of a very hot summer and the circus was standing somewhere near Moreton-in-Marsh. Rebecca said that they might come but that they were haymaking and so it was unlikely that they would leave the farm. The seven o'clock show was full and our little white tent was hot. People piled in, sunburnt, after trips to the nearby pick-your-own strawberry fields or lunch in shady pub gardens. The backstage tent felt heavy and humid. I was sitting by one of the mirrors doing my make-up. Rebecca swung around the corner and into the tent in her tights ready for the show, beaming from ear to ear.

'They are here. I just saw my Uncle Keith. They are all in the middle along the back row.'

I looked through the spy hole in the stage curtain and into the tent. There they were, a row of men all in their best hairy tweed jackets, sweating, but turned out in force to see Rebecca's show.

Rebecca Townsend on Oliver Garrard's grey mare. (James Waddell)

I think that 2002 and 2003 were turning points of sorts. We started to gain confidence. The team changed. Venetia left, sadly; the travellers sort of peeled off and disappeared. The volume of costumes we needed increased and I found a brilliant costume house in Bristol who started fitting, cutting and making for us. We found an American trapeze artiste with a flair for costume and mask making – she made two beautiful furry lion head masks that have roared through the last circus decade without fading. It is surprising how hard costumes and masks are worn, and how many just fall by the wayside over time.

The American trapeze artiste, Emily Park, also did upside-down tap dancing and singing on a trapeze bar, donned in shiny patent shoes, dressed as a 7-year-old girl. She reorganised the wardrobe department, which was at that stage just one very small box wagon, pulling out costumes, repainting the walls, fitting shelves and labelling everything neatly. We found a Russian strongman in Birmingham called Oleg , who came for a season with his pristine physique, his endless mirror gazing, his two mini strongmen boys and their pet Rottweiler. Other characters – a little Dutch woman called Miriam, a tiny Spanish acrobat, two traditional Argentinian drummers (all flashing eyes, long dark hair and dangerous smiles), more dancers, more musicians.

There are winds that blow people across continents, life and fate. This time it was two Ethiopian boys born in Addis Ababa in 1982 and 1983. They learnt to juggle on the streets of Jimma. Their parents sent them to college in England from which they absconded and joined a state-of-the-art London circus school, Circus Space. They heard about an audition for a circus and

Above: American trapeze artiste Emily Park. (James Waddell)

Above left: Emily's lion heads. (James Waddell)

Above right: Rebecca upside down on Gee. (James Waddell)

went to Bristol for the audition. When they arrived in Bristol they called the woman, Nell, who was holding the audition, to learn that the audition was actually in London. Somewhere wires had been crossed – temporarily. They journeyed back to London, to the slick, red-brick audition studio at a circus school in the East End, and there they met a group of English people: Nell, Graham, Toti, Pete and Ian. This group of people didn't speak Ethiopian and the brothers' English was limited, but there was immediately a spark of chemistry.

Bibi and Bichu Tesfamariam were 19 and 20 years old when we met them that day in London. Tall, urban and mesmerisingly beautiful, the brothers juggled handfuls of clubs back-to-back effortlessly and with a charisma that stunned everyone who saw them into jaw-dropped silence. Their juggling was good, very good, but it was

their delivery that stood out – their relaxed grace, their self-possession, their completely natural smiles, the aplomb with which they handled themselves.

We immediately offered them a job with Giffords Circus, wondering how they would take to rural life. I remember meeting them off a bus in Oxford with Toti and driving them out of town along the A40 to our yard. That year, 2002, we were due to open in a field near Cheltenham, just a mile or so from the yard. The tent was already up when the boys arrived. I think we were taking photographs for the programme. My impression of Bibi and Bichu then was of two incredibly well-dressed boys, slightly remote perhaps, slightly intimidating with their dazzling looks. They turned heads everywhere. They walked so slowly, so nonchalantly. They said so little, but projected so much – the very opposite really of so many people.

A gymnast warming up backstage. (James Waddell)

Bibi and Bichu
when we first
met them
in London.
(James
Waddell)

I remember taking them up the field to the tent. They didn't say much but seemed happy, juggling, smiling, and projecting that golden glamour wherever they went. They were dressed in brand-new shining trainers and beautiful mesh sports tops, embroidered with indigo and silver threads. They wore bandanas and mirrored glasses. They didn't seem to mind that they were going to be living in a caravan, in a field, away from the city. They didn't seem to mind anything, they just hung out with Ian Rumbelow of the landscape team, juggling, smiling and dazzling.

I asked Bichu yesterday while we were waiting for the finale, some thirteen years later, what his impressions of us where at that time. He laughed.

'Well, when we went to the circus school in Bristol and we realised it was the wrong place, then we spoke to you and you said you would wait for us, well we thought you must be good people to wait.

'Then we came back to London and met you at Circus Space. Do you remember? We nearly missed you? And then we saw you, in the reception, and you were so many people. We went to that studio upstairs and we juggled for two minutes and you offered us the job, which was great. Then we came to Oxford and you met us with Toti in that old Citroën you had. And then we drove out of Oxford and me and Bibi started to wonder where we were going; we were actually quite worried. We went over the toll bridge out of Oxford and you stopped to pay 5 pence, and by then we were thinking, "what is this?" We had literally never seen that before. And then we went further and further along little roads, far out of Oxford, and me and Bibi were thinking, "where are we? Where are we going?" We actually felt quite scared. Then we arrived at the yard, we saw the tent and we looked inside and it had hay bales! We were thinking, what is this?'

Above: This is Bibi helping me take the babies for a walk in the snow in winter 2010, on the windswept fields between Folly Farm and Cold Aston. (Neil Gifford)

'But you seemed to take it all in your stride as if you weren't worried.'

'Well we have to stay cool, I guess.'

'So why did you stay?'

'Well, we liked you. You took us to the pub and bought us dinner. That was literally the first time we had been to a pub. We felt safe with you, like family. My mum and dad wanted us to visit our cousins every week, which we did, but after we met you we stopped visiting our cousins – we told them, "We have found our own family now".'

Looking back, that seems extraordinarily simple. We liked you. We felt safe with you.

When we opened the show in that drafty muddy field on top of the Cotswold escarpment, despite a horrible dress rehearsal, despite half-built seats, the show was a storming success. Bibi and Bichu were the belles of the ball.

Bibi and Bichu have been with us since then – it is now 2013. They are godparents to our children. They arrive from London with bags full of clothes and toys; they play with the children and look after them. For example, Bichu and I met up in London and went shopping in Westfield Shepherd's Bush. Bichu looked after the children while I whizzed around the shops buying their winter clothes. He took them to a Disney Store and bought them a kind of toy house, and then sat on the concourse playing with the intricate plastic toy house for an hour. If I meet my dad for lunch, or a friend, Bibi and Bichu are always on hand to take the children so that I can talk – and the children are always so happy to see them, dashing across Paddington station and hurling themselves into their outstretched arms. I can't really imagine life without them.

A cousin of mine saw the show this year and was asking me about them. I explained how lovely they were, how integral to the show they are, and supportive with the children. She smiled and said that they looked like me, looked like family. I met Bibi and Bichu in my mid-twenties, when they were in their late teens, so, to some extent I have grown up with them. I was looking at them in the restaurant the other night, and I can say that watching their glowing, open faces, their ready laughs, their poise, their easy way with themselves, I felt a kind of pride that was almost maternal, or at least familial.

They have juggled clubs, rings, hats, they have unicycled, and for our production of War and Peace in 2011 they played marauding French officers juggling knives and fire. Each year they reveal, with an Ethiopian modesty and reserve, a fragment more about themselves and their background. They are the sons of coffee growers. They have a farm in Ethiopia. Their Dad misses them very much. They have a younger brother at home. Bibi has become increasingly involved with the horse department and has learnt to ride and to stand on one of the horses and juggle. Their English is fluent. They call the circus 'their' circus and take an active, and occasionally stern, interest in the day-to-day running of things. Again and again I turn to Bichu when the stress of the show's daily politics overwhelms me, and both he and Bibi are always reassuring and steadying. They whistle and whoop in the finale, always smiling, always with a spring in their step. They know the tent

Watching their glowing, open faces, their ready laughs, their poise, their easy way with themselves, I felt a kind of pride that was almost maternal.

inside out and have a brotherly, affectionate friendship with Toti's landscape team, especially Ian Rumbelow. They are always on hand to dazzle and charm visitors. Many has been the time when, overwhelmed with interval visitors popping in to say hi, I have mouthed 'help' to Bichu, and he and Bibi have strolled over, asked questions and helped to hand round drinks. They have the most impeccable manners, typical Ethiopians; I often wonder if we are in some ways quite coarse and clumsy beside them.

I remember one evening in Hay-on-Wye when the whole company went on a bar crawl around the various pop-up pubs of the festival. I realised that both boys were discreetly making sure that I was looked after within the crowd of drinking people, buying me drinks and not leaving a bar without me. Another time, a slightly suspicious-looking van pulled up overnight in a car park beside the circus. There were some funny-looking men hanging about the van. Surprisingly, this type of thing very rarely happens – the circus seems to be a place that has its own built-in safety warning to potential intruders and, in any case, we are mainly only standing in gentrified rural areas. But on this occasion I did not feel safe while that van was still outside.

Bibi and Bichu walked about the ground all night. In the morning the van had gone.

When the babies were born they came to see me at my home, Folly Farm, in those first two disorientating weeks. Bibi and I went for a walk and he helped me push the pram through the snow, held crying babies, and made cups of tea. The following Christmas, when it snowed for three weeks solid and we were completely snowed in at Folly Farm, to the point where you could not even push the pram across the yard, in-laws, parents and step-parents all came for lunch as everyone's travel plans had been put on hold because of the snow. The babies were crying and I overcooked the turkey and also cried; Bichu arrived and sat calmly in the playroom with the babies, watching football on the telly. He even came to midnight Mass with me, slightly reluctantly – he explained that in Ethiopia his extremely devout mother made them go to church almost daily and on Easter Day they had to go to church for the whole day from early morning until evening, all standing, which had put him off. Nonetheless, in Cold Aston village church, high up in the Cotswolds, amongst the waxy candles and holly branches and tweed-clad families, Bichu's presence at midnight Mass was something akin to one of the three wise kings.

High up in the Cotswolds, amongst the waxy candles and holly branches and tweed-clad families, Bichu's presence at midnight Mass was something akin to one of the three wise kings.

Right: Our box office. (James Waddell)

LONDON

So the company was growing, in size and confidence. Toti and Ian Rumbelow were more confident with the tent and moves. Bibi and Bichu had set a new standard for acts; the glamour of all things unusual – the audience screamed when they came on. Their contact with the public was direct and provocative, but we needed new ways of linking acts. I had been determined from the offset that the circus should be a series of acts that existed in a completely different world to each other, like characters in a cartoon annual, and that the acts should be linked by independently themed dance numbers. This was essentially the Roncalli model and worked for us for a while, but a creative thing has its own life and its own bias; it goes its own way. New people bring new ideas. Conversations excite. In the first few years Kwabana Lindsay did talk to me about workshops and about ensemble but I did not really know what he was talking about, and was resistant to other ways of working. But I was learning the language of creation and theatrical process, and the popularity of the show gave me confidence.

In 2003 we won an award to develop a piece of work. The award was administered by Circus Space and funded by the Jerwood Charitable Foundation. It was prestigious and fairly high profile. Our pitch was to develop a piece of work based on the costumes, movement and language of puppets. I was starting to understand that, good or bad, original or unoriginal, I had a creative instinct, and a drive to create; there is a part of me that is made very happy by thinking, imagining and then realising. I started to spend more time feeding this drive. I now know with a certain confidence that this is an absolutely essential part of the process and that artistes must carve out time to wander, dream, think, be bored, let the mind play over images and be allowed to go where it wants. If the mind wants to search through a big pile of black-and-white postcards at the back of a charity shop in a seaside town, let it. The minions are at work, scurrying about inside the imagination, busy making a thousand tiny little links, odd constructions, playing images against the back of the mind for future use – and they must be allowed this time. If the mind wants to stand and stare at gargoyles around Gloucester Cathedral, let it. Give the creative mind a chance; give it some time and give it some food.

In those early times, excursions with my creative mind were forbidden dates, furtive, secret. I often found myself in Gloucester, searching through dusty shops that just sold comic books, or army surplus, or indoor market pound shops and haberdasher's. The minions love haberdashery almost as much as they love fabric shops: rows of coloured buttons, threads, felts, velvets, stick-on patches and sew-on motifs.

Left: Rebecca as a Scottish doll. (James Waddell)

"you and I, we come from the imagination. And This is like magic. Because if our luck runs out, we can draw something we need and in some way our dreams will come true. *So* <del>Scribble</del>, if your luck runs out, if you desperately need something, then draw it."

In the Beatrix Potter shop in Gloucester – the actual shop of the Tailor of Gloucester – you can climb the little creaky staircase, watch puppet mice sewing in a golden light, and there on the wall is a real Tailor of Gloucester coat with scarlet thread and button holes. Is it real, or is it a book? Is it a tale, or a truth? I love this riddle. Gloucester Cathedral, probably the most famous landmark in the city of Gloucester, is an impressive building that boasts additions in every style of Gothic architecture. When driving into Gloucester, from any direction, the cathedral is the first landmark you see, rising powerfully up from the hilly and swampy landscape. You can just imagine a weary medieval traveller heading to Gloucester and spotting the cathedral tower in the distance, topped by its four delicate pinnacles, and imagine the relief and emotion that it must have evoked. It is an epic building: the dank cloisters; the sweet cloister garden; the threadbare flags; the angel orchestra. These are the things

I love there: the angel orchestra in the roof that you can look at by staring down into a mirror that faces the vaulted ceiling; the figure of Robert Curthose, eldest son of William the Conqueror, carved from coloured bog oak, polished, pointy toed, with lurchers at his feet; the painted wall carvings portraying local noble families; and a couple with heavy dark cloaks and ruffs, sitting opposite each other in prayer, with their seventeen children represented, kneeling in rows behind them. When the babies were born we took them there for their first outing, and they were christened there in 2010, in the Lady Chapel.

I discovered that the cathedral had housed an art installation that involved horses. I found this work very exciting. The cathedral had allowed the then artist-in-residence to walk two horses around the cathedral all night for two nights, and for the event to be filmed. The artist had then made a film from this footage. I watched a little screen in one of the cloisters that was

Above: Imagining Pierrot. (Nell Gifford)

Right: The fragments that make up a show. (Nell Gifford)

showing the film, the slow echoing step of the horses, their cautious investigation of the space, their breath, their stops and starts, their curiously respectful attitude to the cathedral interior, seeing it as a refuge, or stable. Horses inside. Horses in a city. Horses as theatre. The minions were having a busy day that day.

On another occasion I found myself wandering around a strange rickety place called Gloucester Folk Museum, one of the oldest established museums dedicated to social history, housed in a complex of Tudor buildings that to this day still show evidence of the wattle-and-daub style of architecture and beautiful original wall paintings. It was within this Aladdin's cave of old wooden farm machinery, 1950s kitchen appliances, children's toys from a range of eras, relics from local folklore, stuffed farm animals, seventeenth-century homeware and costumes, delicate pin-making machines and magnificent paintings depicting local life, that I discovered the work of an early arts and crafts artist called William Simmonds. The staff at the museum said that there was an entire collection of important William Simmonds puppets in the museum archive, which could be viewed if I made an appointment.

The next day I climbed up the slippery wooden stairs past the rows of mechanical animals and historical dolls into the annex of the timber-framed building. The curator unfolded a table beside a pile of thick cardboard boxes and started to slowly unwrap the puppets from their tissue beds. I felt a rush of blood around my body, a feeling as if I couldn't breathe. Something in my mind went into overdrive. How long had it taken

to find the Simmonds puppets? A long search, but there they were, in these boxes in this dark attic all along.

They were so beautiful. Columbine in a net skirt trimmed in pink. A white horse that cantered and reared. A strange, dark-blue wizard with a hunchback. Woodland creatures, elves and goblins, a fawn with conker-smooth limbs, tufty hair and little horns. A red-lipped Pierrot. Each figure was a marionette and precisely engineered to have a distinct movement language of its own: Columbine was on her tip toes; the hunchback nodded as it walked; the horse had perfectly articulated knee and fetlock joints. Each was made and used by William Simmonds during the 1920s and 1930s, from his shows Circus, Harlequinade and his most famous, The Woodland.

The funding award had been granted to Giffords Circus to work with three performers over a period of time to develop a piece of performance. I was learning the ropes of being a producer – fitting artistes to timescales, the timescales to budgets, and meeting a deadline. In this case the artistes were Rebecca Townsend, Emily Park, the little American trapeze artiste-cum-costumier, and a third girl, Isabelle Woywode.

Izzy, who had been born and raised in Berlin, was a trained dancer and aerial performer. I think we met her at an audition at Circomedia in Bristol. She was there to support a friend. I can say that the friend was forgettable … but Izzy was unforgettable. She had huge blue eyes, sunshine and rainbow eyes – crazy eyes – and an equally huge smile. She was a well-trained jazz, tap and ballet dancer

I felt a rush of blood around my body, a feeling as if I couldn't breathe. Something in my mind went into overdrive. How long had it taken to find the Simmonds puppets?

Left: A William Simmonds puppet. (Nell Gifford)

but her huge imagination had taken her up onto the trapeze and into the skies. She is one of those performers who will never slack off when onstage, never do glazed, or mechanical, or below par, but just gives completely of themselves – a performer that will die rather than not do. A performer that is sort of consuming themselves in the process – tough, experienced, but still frail, as they daily wrench out of themselves everything they physically have for their work. She was fun to work with as well.

So Izzy, Rebecca, Emily and myself spent about two months in a village hall trying to carve out three doll characters. We worked and worked at it. We played music, we danced and played dressing-up with a massive pile of old costumes. Slowly, the characters started to form. We went to London and worked with a director who had studied with Jacques Lecoq in Paris. He had his own system of creating character through movement. We worked with him in his studio for days. We worked with the neutral mask – a plain mask worn over the face, which works by neutralising the facial expressions and in the process reveals all the character that is expressed by the body. We worked with Commedia dell'Arte characters. We developed long improvisation exercises using the body, the voice and movement. It was a world that I did not know anything about; the science of movement, the breaking down of movement into a thousand exacting theatrical expressions, and the slow process of building character from nothing.

The work in that studio was in some ways very depressing. We did not feel as if we were getting anywhere. I made a mistake, a big mistake with hindsight, which was that I did not participate. I watched and filmed. I think that this set up an odd dynamic in the room. At one point Emily was arguing with the director about something and he flipped, started shouting at us

all and said that in all his time he had never met anyone so unco-operative. Afterwards he told me that he had seen that happen before, when the actor becomes so locked down that they cannot move at all. To me, then, it seemed quite terrifying and I felt an overwhelming responsibility for these three performers to lead them and look after them. I know now that the set-up in a rehearsal or workshop room is so vital to the development of any production. A slightly strange feeling can derail the whole process. It has to be solid and safe. I think everyone in the room has to be participating or leading. Silent observers contribute more than they think.

We went back to the circus and continued to rehearse. Rebecca's character was Scottish, she danced a Scottish reel, and leapt off the back of her horse. Emily was a kind of sickly sweet, singing, kitsch cowgirl and Izzy was a puppet doll aerialist.

The work we produced was all right. The costumes were good. The horse work was very good. The three girls played their parts to the full. Know this – if you buy it, the audience will buy it. But something was missing. The movement I had given them, and that we had mutually decided upon, was too normal. The movement style did not really evoke anything. We were on our way to selecting and producing some truly great horse performances. We had a distinct style of costume and were learning fast how to produce good costumes and how to keep them sharp on the road, but my stage direction was not good enough. I was good at an initial vision. I was good at building excitement onstage in broad brush strokes of performers and music combined, but the tighter direction of the artistes, the one-to-one work, the director/choreographer role – I was really floundering.

I remember another circus director or critic coming to see the show and remarking that it lacked a strong directorial hand.

We had been praised a lot. We had had a lot of good reviews, and mine and Toti's vision had been eulogised about in the local press. Giffords Circus as a whole had built a name for being beautiful, charming, romantic and inspired. But it was not this I heard at all. Negative feedback sounds much louder, and rightly so.

Izzy was so supportive. She was in some ways more experienced in show production than I was.

'Don't worry so much, Nell,' she said one evening, when we had just opened. We were playing at an arts centre called Taurus Crafts in the Forest of Dean. I remember this moment sharply. I was feeling low and paranoid, unsure of my place within the company. The River Severn glowed in the distance and in the foreground was a vast timber bull, a Trojan horse that the arts centre volunteers had built. The bull loomed above us. The river flowed. Izzy's voice was right beside me.

'Don't worry. Don't worry. You have got a great team here. They believe in you. Don't worry.'

Those words, on that day, helped a lot.

We needed expertise, and I think that, subconsciously, this is why we decided to take the show to London.

We were a company that was used to leafy lanes, muddy gateways, dark nights, village pubs. A circus-move night smells of diesel, crushed grass, Red Bull and coffee. We are used to arriving in silent sleeping villages, our engines roar, cutting through velvety night and hooting owls.

In London it was totally different. We drove from Brighton festival to London. In those days we used to drive in one long convoy. I say drive … most of the time the entire convoy was parked up on the motorway hard shoulder. Everything that could

break down did. I remember sitting in the cab of a car watching as Ian Rumbelow and Toti, followed by Bibi and Bichu, ran the length of the convoy carrying a battery each. We sat there on the hard shoulder for hours, until somehow the convoy was pushed, jumpstarted, hotwired and siphoned into motion. We roared and sputtered into London, little painted burgundy caravans bouncing behind old Land Rovers, tiny toys under the looming high-rise of the City.

We arrived in Old Street at about five o'clock in the morning. We were threading our way from Old Street onto Hoxton Square. The convoy was blocking the rush-hour traffic coming down Old Street and into the City. Every minute the traffic increased and with it the pressure on us to get out of the way. We were going to stand on Hoxton Square. There was nowhere else for us to park and so, until we opened the gates to the square and started getting the vehicles on, there was nowhere for the painted caravans, old Land Rovers, wagons and lorries to go. We had been given the backyard of Circus Space for the horses and had luckily managed to get the horse wagon in ahead of the main convoy. The stable team started building the stables, heavy stable panels and sledge hammers ringing like bells against the tarmac. Then somebody put their head out of a garret window.

'Will you lot please stop making so much bloody noise, what time is it anyway?!'

'Sorry we have to put the stables up.'

But there were no spare hands to gently lift the stable panels off the horse lorry, for every spare person was helping Toti to get the gates to the square open. The convoy was still blocking the road and a huge traffic gridlock was building up around it. Any minute now we would be on the travel news. We would be costing the economy millions as workers could not get into the offices. It was half past five. Horns were blowing. Engines were revving.

Pushing the first wagon
onto Hoxton Square,
Shoreditch, London, 6 a.m.
(James Waddell)

Finally, we got the gates to the square unlocked. We started to push the first wagon in. We realised then that our measurements were out. Hoxton Square is a very small city square anyway and it was going to be tight. But not, we had hoped, this tight. We simply could not fit the wagon through the gateway, as the steel hinges of the gate were sticking out. Time was ticking; it was nearly six o'clock. We were still stuck all the way down Old Street. Not one vehicle had moved.

I was at the front of the first wagon, near to Toti who was shouting instructions to the team who pushed and pulled the wagon into place.

'OK, stop everyone. At the back, hold it!'

The wagons are heavy and require people to run with wooden blocks to secure the wheels while others hold them steady. In this case the camber of the pavement ran on a downward slope from the gates to the little tree-lined square, and if the wagon rolled it would crash into the tightly parked cars on the opposite curb.

'Hold it, blocks! Block the back wheels!'

Toti had sweat pouring down his face, into his eyes and off his top lip. He was swearing quietly and thinking hard.

'Think, Toti, think,' he was muttering. Blasts of horns, shouts and revs from the main road.

'Damn, just do it,' he muttered.

Toti is incredibly strong; he has a reserve of strength, for when it is needed. He turned around and lifted the end panel by the side of the gate. With one careful

Above: It was a week that we all decided to have our hair cut. This is Rebecca sitting outside on the square. The clown, Luca, was also a hairdresser. (Nell Gifford)

heave he lifted the gate post and the panel straight out of the concrete. He placed the panel gently against the adjacent panel. The gap was now wide enough for all the wagons. With a cheer, the first wagon was pushed up the pavement, over the curb and onto the grass of Hoxton Square.

There was magic in the air that week. The caretakers of the park were good-natured about the missing panel, and at the end of the week Toti replaced it so you would never have known it had been removed. They welcomed the horse manure, old straw and hay bedding. They loved seeing the horses out in front of the circus, grazing in front of the White Cube Gallery and they told us that the atmosphere of Hoxton changed a bit while we

were there. They said that people were calmer, and they thought it was because of the presence of the horses. Adam Ant came to every show with his daughter and wrote us a fan letter.

For a week we were Hoxton locals. It was early in the regeneration of the East End and the streets were buzzing. We were used to playing in villages and fields where there was little or no security threat. This felt very different, and so we hired a local security firm to help look after the circus equipment. We had done this before, elsewhere, and we had had to specify how many personnel we wanted and for how long. The Cheltenham security firm had sent one man who slept all night in his car outside the ground,

Note in the left image (handwritten fan letter):

ADAM ANT
24/5/03
Dear Everyone at Giffords Circus.

Your show is 1000% times better than Cirque de Soleil! (or any other for that matter - And I have seen quite a few.)

My daughter, Lily Caitlin + myself were Spell-bound for 2 hours. Every child should have the chance to see a true, spectacular, passionate circus like yours. Simply Excellent! B·R·E·A·T·H·-·T·A·K·-·I·N·G! Pure dedication, skill + practice delivered with grace, humour +

undisturbed by the comings and goings of the circus folk. In Brighton, the festival had supplied security guards as there were active animal rights protesters in Brighton who turned out for all circus shows. The Brighton festival guards were big camp blokes with matching bomber jackets, friendly and a part of the festival scene. This was very different. In the East End we paid a fee and the company sent out as much security as they thought necessary. I got the feeling that the boys they sent were hopping from one job to the other, roving gangs who would go en masse to a location if trouble flared up. The guys they sent didn't say anything. They looked like men who did not sleep. They looked truly dangerous.

The cost of the security, the hire of the ground, the cost of moving all the vehicles in and out of town, and keeping the circus supplied with hay and straw, diesel and gas meant that we lost money in London. But in some ways, it did not matter. We had taken our rural show to a metropolitan audience in a capital city. This experience showed up our weaknesses. It was a tough, unindulgent, critical audience, in some cases an audience that wanted to get its hands on us and bend us into something better, and that was just what we needed. From this audience of Circus Space staff, contemporary circus practitioners, funders, arts council executives, fashionable East End families, multicultural, stylish and rich in open-top sports cars, fashion stylists, actors and London circus people, emerged two people who persuaded us to allow them to get their hands on us. Who gave willingly of what they knew. Who understood us well enough to be able to help. Who had an instinct for grass roots circus, for stubborn little companies like us determined to reinvent the wheel, who were in desperate need of help but too shy or proud to accept it.

Those two people were Barry Grantham and Angela de Castro.

Above left: The fan letter from Adam Ant. (Giffords Circus collection)

Above right: Emily Park. (James Waddell)

Right: Poster from 2002. (Drawn by Endellion Lycett Green)

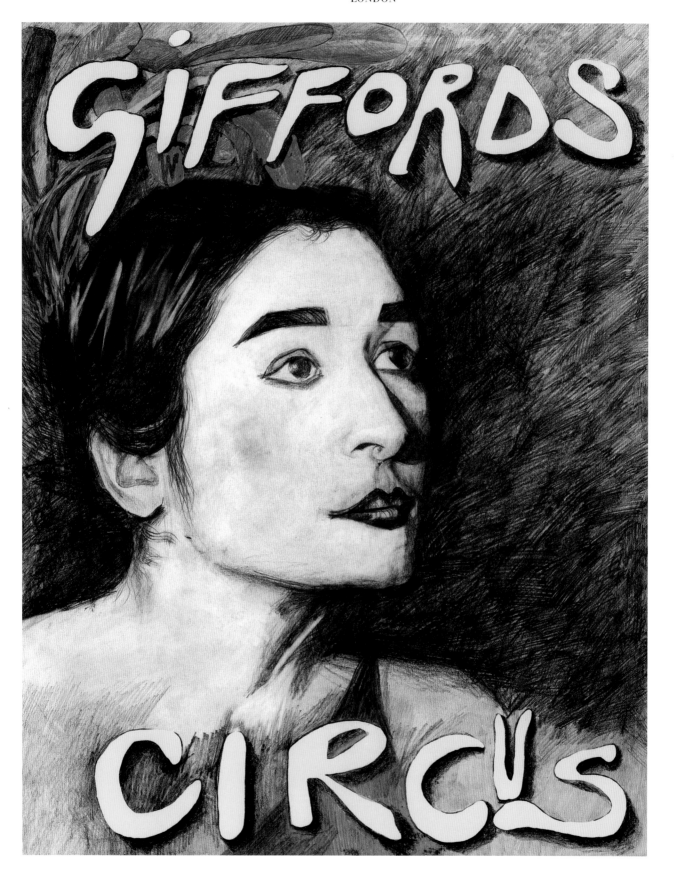

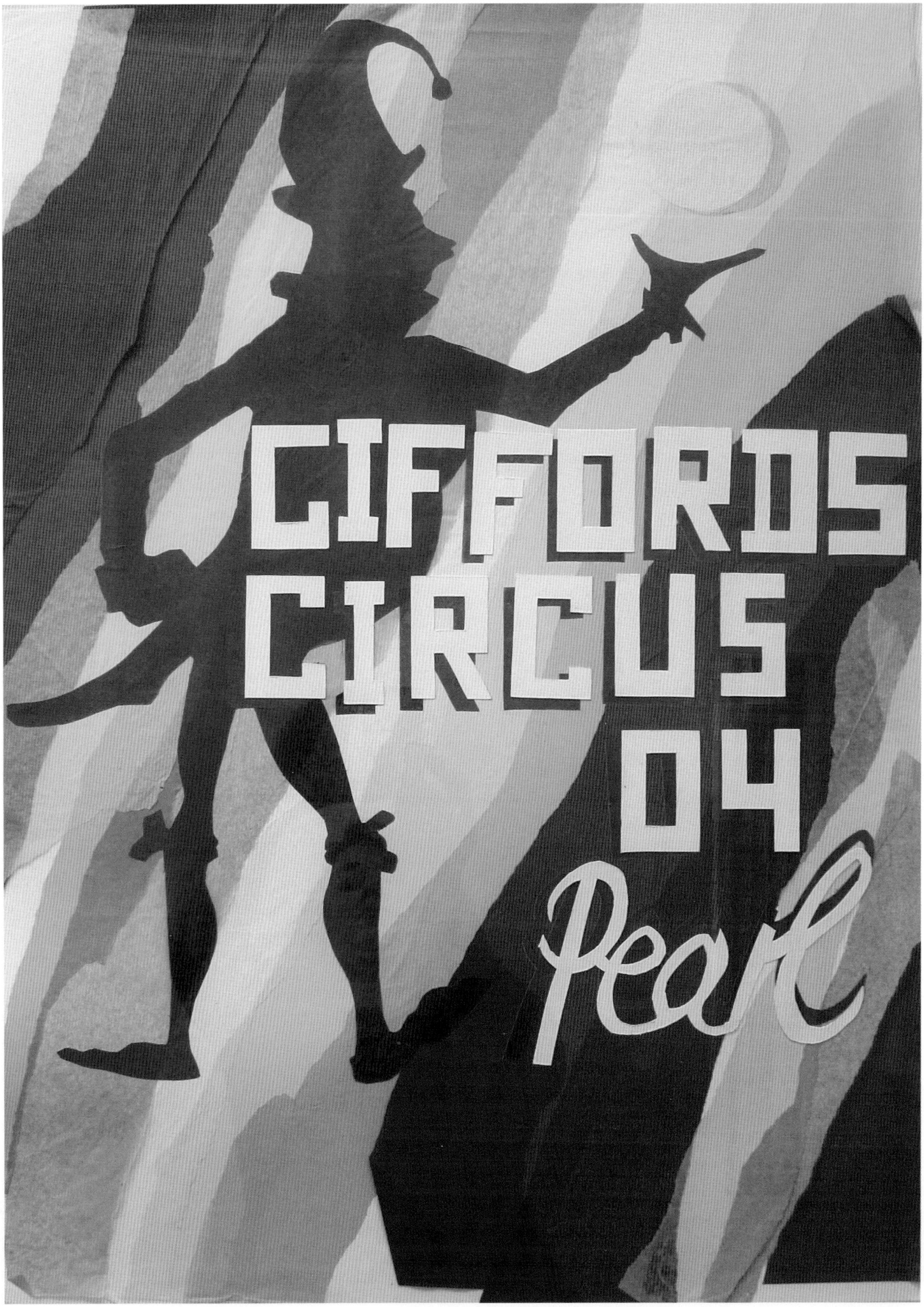
GIFFORDS
CIRCUS
04
Pearl

5

FROGS, PEARLY QUEENS AND PIERROTS

Barry Grantham is as old as Drury Lane and as sprightly as Pan. He is a performer, director, and he teaches Commedia dell'Arte, which is a sixteenth-century Italian style of improvisation and performance. The popular characters Harlequin, Columbine and Pantaloon come from Commedia. Barry is an expert in the Commedia styles and skills – the mimes, movements and masks. His maternal grandfather was a music-hall artiste and his father a classical actor. Barry trained as a dancer with Idzikowski, a famous Harlequin in the Diaghilev Company, and was coached by him for that role. A hundred years of dance and theatre. He has worked in almost every form of theatre, from fringe to the West End, and in films such as *The Red Shoes* and *The Tales of Hoffman*. He and his wife Joan work constantly, touring, performing, teaching – they travel to Norway, Sweden, Holland, Germany and Italy giving masterclasses, dancing, delighting – entertainers absolutely to the core, to the end and from the beginning. Joan plays the piano. Barry dances. He is an elderly man but I have seen him lift, carry, sweep students off their feet, dance for hours on end, instructing, pointing, grimacing, watching.

Barry was also a friend of Tweedy, our new clown, and I remember Tweedy explaining about eccentric dance, one of Barry's specialties:

They are old music hall steps, comic dance, and are actually hard to learn. They are the sort of thing you see in old Disney cartoons – hops, skips, twisting leaps, the body goes at funny angles. It's a type of grotesque 'rubber-limbed' dance. Steps like Snake Hips, The Shimmy, The Cup and Saucer, The Lambeth Walk. No one really teaches eccentric dance now.

Tweedy's little demonstrations of some of the steps intrigued me.

'I think he would choreograph the show for you as well.'

Tweedy gave me Barry's contact details and I called him. An old-sounding crackly voice answered the London telephone number.

'Hello?'

'Hello, I am so sorry to bother you but I am Nell Gifford and Tweedy gave me your number. I was wondering if you could help me with my show, Giffords Circus. We have been going for four years. We tour in the Cotswolds.'

'Ah yes. Tweedy was mentioning something about this. Yes, yes, When are you rehearsing?'

Barry and I met in the cafe at The Royal Academy. Barry is small and bird-like, with beady eyes. He listens harder than he talks. He has a loud, crackly laugh, a very grand English accent. We walked around an exhibition of couture fashion – I think it was Christian Dior. We talked about the

Left: Pearl poster, 2004. (Drawn by Endellion Lycett Green)

Berner Tagblatt, 25.6.1919

show. I said that it was called The Pearl, and that it was new departure for us to give the show a name – in the past it had simply been Giffords Circus 2000, 2001, 2002 and 2003. Miriam, the little gypsy lady with the big black horse, was returning, along with her brigand boyfriend. They would be playing pirates; I had an idea about a moon, a pearl and Pierrot. The show felt watery, dark, moonlit. Sometimes I feel that putting a show together is like trying to read the future – as if the show is already formed and you are feeling your way towards it in the dark. I wanted to create a kind of frog prince character, inspired by the song 'A frog he would a-wooing go'. My sister Clover had suggested using the Disney song 'Everybody wants to be a cat' for the finale. I played the song constantly to myself. I did that a lot in those early days – playing songs over and over to myself, accessing an identical emotion or reaction each time, and in the slow understanding

of that emotion, sort of solidifying it so that I could use it in the show.

In the Royal Academy we drank coffee; people came and went. Barry said that he could work very fast if he needed to on the choreography. He told me about a time when he worked in a studio putting together routines for a show. They had four different groups of girls and one piano, so they had to rotate the girls around the room, each getting half an hour or so with the piano. He laughed affectionately remembering the other choreographer, Madam Laurant, in her pencil skirt and high heels and no-nonsense way with the girls.

'She could dance all day in those heels, always so smart,' he said, and he laughed his crackly laugh.

He said that he would like to spend some time with the company doing eccentric dance and holding a Commedia workshop. I agreed although, secretly, I was not exactly sure what he was talking about. I showed

Above: Pierrot research. (Giffords Circus collection)

him some of my drawings, which he seemed to really like. It was the first time I had ever really shown any of my drawings of a show to anyone, and it was like oxygen to hear from Barry that he thought they were good. (He is always polite, but is never fake and is often extremely critical.) I felt so encouraged. We talked about the finale. I said that I liked it when the whole company joined in for the finale, and he agreed. He said that he could work on this. We talked about the pearl, and what it was and how it would be represented in the show. A dream of a pearl – the centre of a show.

Somewhere along the way we talked about the time he would spend with us – I think that the initial suggestion was about a week. We agreed a fee. We talked about the rehearsal space. I explained that we had started to use a village hall about 2 miles from Folly Farm, where we now lived, called Notgrove Village Hall. Barry said that it should be fine, so long as it was

dry, the floor was flat and preferably made of wood.

Barry Grantham alighted from the train at 10.15 a.m. at Kingham station on a Wednesday morning in early spring, amongst a farmer returning for a mid-week break in London, some Japanese tourists clutching maps of Bourton-on-the-Water, the odd race horse trainer, and some blonde-haired girls with gappy teeth. Barry, neat in his blue tracksuit, carrying his kit bag, walking the way he does – a dancer's walk, toes pointed out, heels never really touching the ground. Smiles and hugs and no, he is fine with his bag. We drove back to Folly Farm, through Bourton. He asked me again about the pearl, and what it was. I remember not really knowing at all, and saying that the pearl was an offstage force. I remember feeling panicky that I didn't know. The genesis of a show – the balance of leaving room but being prepared. Ideas will grow in a rehearsal room, but the

company needs to be confident and that comes from planning and leadership. I am used to this feeling now, the pressure to get that balance right, to have the answer while I keep asking the questions – but I was green then, green and nervous, although thankfully, though I didn't quite realise, in the hands of a master.

We arrived at Folly Farm, drove down the poplar tree-lined drive, into the yard and up to the doors of the main barn, which were open. The barn was up even if the gabled ends were still sheeted. We had hung Izzy's hoop in the barn and she was sitting on it, ready to practise.

'What a lovely sight that is,' crackled Barry, clapping his hands. 'Splendid!'

He stopped to look around Folly Farm briefly. Barry changed into his training clothes, and then we drove the mile or so to the next-door village of Notgrove. Notgrove is a pretty, estate-run Cotswold village, high on the top of the Cotswold Edge – a limestone escarpment that forms the eastern edge of the valley of the Severn. The hall has a little bar and fortnightly country and western evenings. The hall itself was built in 1958 by the Anderson family and is actually a reclaimed hall, which was originally in the East End of London. I found this out recently and thought that this was a rather extraordinary fact. Over the years we have rehearsed a great deal of material in that little wooden building, and much of the material might easily have come from the East End, *c.* 1940. It is almost as if the hall *was* a music hall, and had its own agenda, its own need to keep producing piano rags and tap breaks, eccentric dance and close harmony.

A serious, hilarious, genius, full-time clown. Mercurial, maverick, reading an audience with a brain that moves as fast as a fish.

We arrived in Notgrove, parked and crossed the little road to the hall, waiting for a tractor and a Land Rover to pass. We walked into the hall foyer, past the photographs of the village cricket team and the country and western evenings. The company was already in the hall, waiting for us. The musicians had set up the keyboard and the drums: Bill, with his blonde locks and Viking looks; Colin, neat and serious behind the piano; Peter Sen on the drums. There were a couple of the front-of-house girls, and Tweedy, Nancy, Rebecca and Izzy. They were ready for us.

Two more people had joined Giffords Circus, two people who would – by their instinct and charisma and imagination – help mould the company for years to come. They were Alan Digweed, otherwise known, and always known, as Tweedy the clown, and Nancy Trotter, a local girl who wanted to run away with the circus.

Originally from Aberdeen, Tweedy is a very fit, extraordinary man who wanted to be a cartoonist and then decided in his late teens to instead turn himself into a cartoon character. He has worked in all of the circus shows in the UK – I first met him in Glasgow way back when I was riding elephants and mucking-out horses, and he was young, wild and drunk. Since then he gave up drinking following an accident falling off a unicycle and became a serious, hilarious, ingenious, full-time clown. Mercurial, maverick, reading an audience with a brain that moves as fast as a fish, he cuts to the heart of people's sense of self, their embarrassment, their longings, their need to be laughed at, sent up,

pomposity exploding in the air in a bang of foam and flour. A man who can represent onstage the frustration of things, a struggle with a world that tangles all about him as he tries to sort it out, that defeats him – but in that defeat there is a triumph. Tweedy is one of the most hardworking, clever, kind people you could ever meet. He is always prepared – he comes to each project ready with ideas, photographs, YouTube clips, DVDs. He manages to get into every meeting but is never unwanted. He makes the room lighter, the project more achievable. He is very strong, muscly, with a dry, iron-hard body of well-worked muscles, a cartoon face that can twist into any shape, and a shaved head with a Tintin tuft of bright red hair. His hands and feet seem to have been put on at odd angles, and he runs with no rhythm at all but like a foal, sort of trotting and cantering at the same time, as if it is the first time he has run. Tweedy, in his orange boiler suit, is the first person up on

a move day, cap on, cracking jokes, hands behind his back, like an old man and a child at the same time. He runs down the road at the end-of-year party saying goodbye, dressed as a duckling; backstage, resting, eating from his chocolate box he puts a fake fish on his head before getting back to work. Tweedy was friends with Barry and had worked with him before joining us in 2004. They greeted each other as old friends.

Nancy is a tall, beautiful girl with a soul as old as the hills. Emily Park once said, 'Gad Nancy, you are so goddam beautiful but you are not a bitch. How do you do it?' And it was true – you can't imagine a more serious and self-questioning person. When we had advertised an audition for company members, I kept getting messages from a very serious, if somewhat disorganised-sounding, girl. Messages like,

'Oh gosh, oh gosh, I hope it's not too late. I so want to audition!'

Click. No name, No number.

Above: Tweedy at work. (Nell Gifford)

Right: Gerald and Tweedy. (James Waddell)

The next day: 'I am in Scotland. I so hope it is not too late. Oh God, I think it is …'

Click. No name.

The voice sounded so earnest, so genuinely wanting to be a part of the company and so, well – nice. Somehow Nancy found her way to our yard. The tall beautiful teenager who gamely wire-brushed the under carriages of wagons, swept the yard, sold candy floss, and did just about every last thing that was asked of her with an incredible grace and good nature, a beautiful duckling, is now, in 2013, a swan. There are lots of teenagers who think that they want the circus, think that it is for them, but there are very few who go the distance like Nancy has – many years on tour with us, many roles, many tiny caravans, many late moves, many dark nights, many rehearsal days, two years at a terrifying acting school in Paris where they tear you apart before reconstructing you as a silent performer – Nancy has danced, performed grotesque, mimed, sung, acted, trained doves – she has emerged as an extraordinary world-class artiste and comic.

> There are lots of teenagers who think that they want the circus, think that it is for them, but there are very few who go the distance like Nancy.

There were others that year, but I had worked out a formula, a formula that I would later understand to be deeply problematic for the company. This formula was a core of company members – Izzy, Tweedy, Rebecca, Nancy, and Peter Sen the drummer, plus two other male musicians – that were joined later in the rehearsal period by the artistes – the strong man, the woman with the big black horse, some Kenyan acrobats, and so on. This approach divided the company, and prevented us from becoming a true ensemble – an issue that I would not understand until a new director, de Castro, joined us a year later. For the time being we were concerned with finding great artistes and learning about choreography.

Early in the spring Toti and I had visited Romania with a good friend of ours called Graham Thomas. Graham is an ageless son of the circus, an ex-lion-tamer and juggler who has run wild-animal departments, toured the USA, lived on trains and performed with the best in the world. He now lives near Oxford, making and hiring out marquees. He is funny, quick-witted, discreet and modest. He has an old-fashioned transatlantic way: for example, addressing Toti's father – to whom Toti introduced him recently – as 'sir'. He is highly experienced in the business of circus and was, miraculously, willing to help us.

He, Toti and I had ventured to Bucharest where Graham had Romanian contacts. Christy, a Romanian contact of Graham's, met us at the airport and we were quickly joined by another of his friends. Word got round that we were in town, and I think the word was that we were there to do business in the widest sense. The truth was that we were there to find a circus act. But before we could get to the circus building our entourage grew, and before we knew it a group of puffa jacket-clad boys with smoky cars and mobile phones in each pocket were taking us to the iron works and concrete factories, to empty offices lined in marble. We looked at pressed metal outdoor furniture and visited back-yard factories where families welded seating stands in their gardens. One of the puffas tried to sell us the family

Some of my
drawings
towards The
Pearl Show.
(Nell Gifford)

Rebecca on Ronan. (James Waddell)

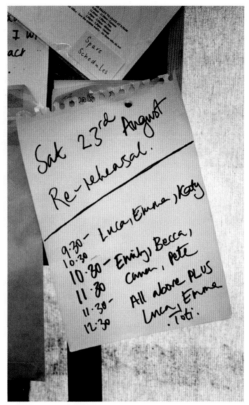

as well as the welding work. It was very uncomfortable and frightening. We went down dark alleys, very dark alleys, to offices where we were being offered a trade in anything we wanted. Wherever we went the puffa jackets came too, smoking, checking their mobiles. It was free-trade Romania. There was no middle class, just very poor people or very rich people. Bucharest was a city of casinos, cheap gold and crime. We visited one factory floor and as we walked through, the proprietor switched off a radio that a group of workers were listening to.

'Gypsies,' nodded one of the puffas. 'No gypsy music allowed here. It causes trouble.'

Frustrated by two days of viewing empty factories, Graham, Toti and I reconvened at the Intercontinental Hotel and plotted how we could get to the circus building. The puffas were our only answer. We could not shake them off, and we did not speak Romanian. We went out on the town that night to the casinos and had an incredible string of luck on the cards playing blackjack. A sign. The next day we asked the puffas if we could go into the huge Romanian State Circus building. Nods, smiles, a lot of talk in Romanian. No problem, no problem. My brother works there. My girlfriend is an artiste. Come this way. Once inside the large, 1930s purpose-built municipal circus building we were able to stroll through the marble-floored corridors and look into the rehearsal rooms and studios. We saw a beautiful girl doing backwards somersaults onto her partner's shoulders. The puffas were circling us, watching our every move. I was sweaty and shaking. How could we get to talk to this mesmerising flashing-eyed couple with

Above: Performance and rehearsal – The Pearl Show in full swing. (Giffords Circus collection; James Waddell)

the perfect line? The girl rocketed through the air to land on her partner's head. A tiny glamorous woman shouted instructions to them from the ground. Graham watched them. 'Good,' he said, nodding. I nodded. The puffas came closer. They were putting their mobile phones away. If we made a move they would be in for the kill, driving the price sky high and muddying the potential relationship between us and the artistes. If we stood there at the door to the studio for much longer the puffas would realise that we were interested. And if we moved on, we might never find our way back, might never see the couple again. It was now or never. It felt as if going home empty-handed would be the end of things.

'Hey, Nell,' Graham suddenly said, loudly and slowly, 'do you want to see the animals, look at the zoo?'

'OK, yes, great, yes please.'

'Hey guys, which way is the zoo?' Graham and I started to move. Toti realised what Graham was doing and came with us, only at the back of the group, and then he sank back into a doorway, out of view. Graham and I made a big deal of seeing the zoo, waving and asking the puffas to show us this and that. The decoy worked. The puffas took us on and through the building, leaving Toti to quietly approach and speak to the artistes. He got a phone number.

We had ourselves an act. We met Evelyn and Christian Marinof the next day at the hotel to discuss the contract. They were very well-educated urbane circus performers – Evelyn was training to be a barrister, Christian was a professional gymnastics coach. They agreed to come to England for a season, and later that trip we met their

families and feasted on plates of cheese, meat and red wine, Romanian high style.

When I presented Barry to the company waiting for us in the hall, Barry said hello to everyone. They were polite and a little nervous. Expectation hung the air. Leading a group, directing, choreographing is in some ways more nerve-wracking than performing. The rehearsal room looks at you. You have to be ready. You have to be open, you have to know and not know at the same time. It is so easy to feel intimidated, to stumble. In those early days I often just simply did not know what to do in rehearsal – or rather, I didn't trust myself well enough to think that what I wanted to do was any good. I did not know what Barry was going to do either, but I do remember feeling

intensely grateful that there was somebody else there with me who was in charge.

Barry walked about the hall in his trainers clutching his little wrinkly hands to his chest, muttering to himself and looking at the floor. He then suddenly said, 'Right, come on,' in his elegant crackly voice, and gathered the performers around him. He kept taking little beady glances at them. They stood around him, watching his every move. Everyone was smiling. Everyone's faces were open and expectant. He already had the group in his hand and he had apparently done nothing.

He then took the group through a series of hand and body gestures. How to invite with one hand, how to dismiss, the hand curling towards you as the arms cascade downward from the shoulder, or the arm climbing upwards with the hand flicking away from the body in a series of rolls.

Above and right: Izzy as Pierrot. (James Waddell; Giffords Circus collection)

How to look with the whole body, the upper body moving from side to side while the shoulders stay totally level and the hips motionless. Double takes. He made us play games, still standing in a circle: the game of Ha!; Silly Noises and Silly Walks; Glee!; Make Yourself Laugh; Harlequin Knees Bend; Smart Walking; and Harlequin Hears No Good of Himself. Barry's face was in turn surprised, quizzical, confused, cross and flirtatious as he worked through the gestures, often breaking into his crackly laugh of approval when somebody pleased him. Embarrassment fell away as the group saw the challenge of each game and wanted to please Barry, to do it well – neatly, concisely, humorously. Barry in his pale blue tracksuit, pale sunlight filtering through the windows, the quiet village outside, the hall warm and snug, a sense of having time to work stuff out – precious moments.

He worked very closely with Izzy on the Pierrot character. He showed her how to hold an invisible pearl. Finger and thumb, hold, lift and turn. Izzy played with the invisible pearl, bouncing it from hand to hand, throwing it to Tweedy – like the magic, the pearl became a real pearl. Look, look and look away. The double take. We worked with an umbrella – magic and mime – learning how to make a character appear and disappear behind a spinning umbrella. Barry had an umbrella on his shoulder, kicking steps forward, lifted and dropped the umbrella in front of him, dragging it backwards with little shuffling steps.

Barry punctuated a series of steps with exclamations, accents and punch words.

'Ah rum pa PAH! Ah rum pa PAH! – kick and oppositional hands on the PAH everyone!'

He would call to the performers marching eagerly behind him – and the room

Left: Izzy as Pierrot. (Giffords Circus collection)

Above: Barry dancing with Toti and me in the finale. Dress by Vivienne Westwood, since then handed onto nieces for their cabaret shows. (Giffords Circus collection)

followed with every fibre of their bodies, minds and hearts. And Barry was very, very funky. He could choreograph some of the fastest, wildest, most absurd routines you can ever imagine. Peter Sen and his two new musicians were all well trained and could thrash out just about any tune you pointed them towards, in great high style. The hall that rocked. The music hall. Izzy gestured, Tweedy danced like a newborn lamb on magic mushrooms, Rebecca strutted and cartwheeled, the band rocked out. I sat in the corner, writing furiously, occasionally stopping Barry to suggest an idea for the narrative – to direct I suppose – and Barry danced between us, the maestro.

What I learnt in that hall that year was that the relationship between director and choreographer is key. I learnt as well that if you have good performers and a good choreographer you can work *fast*. The work I did with the three girls was I think, looking back on it now, a kind of reception class. It was the start of learning – a foundation. We

had worked very slowly. Now, with The Pearl Show, we were churning out routines and dance sequences – more than we could ever use. It was breathtakingly exciting. I remember working with the band on the old English nursery rhyme 'A frog he would a-wooing go'. We did a classic nursery-style version of it and then, under my direction and with the boys' musical brilliance, twisted it off into a classical version, a punk version, each new style triggering the performers into different dance styles. Experiments with urgency.

That year there was an extraordinary alchemy between Izzy and Tweedy. In 'Everybody wants to be a cat' Tweedy and Izzy danced like demons, Tweedy dressed as a sort of Tintin pearly queen and Izzy as Pierrot. At one point she did a high kick sideways, appearing to comically knock Tweedy backwards, all set at a breakneck speed with Barry's electric moves, music-hall jives and comic steps.

Finally we were finding a movement language of our own.

'Everybody wants to be a cat'. The finale. Rocking the tent in the 2004 show The Pearl. Finally we were finding a movement language of our own. (Giffords Circus collection)

6

THE CIRCUS HAS A HOME

The single biggest problem for us in running the circus was the fact that we did not have a base, a headquarters, a 'farm' – as all circus headquarters tend to be called, whether they are agricultural or not.

We lived in the yard at Severn Springs for two long winters. I don't think the visceral memory of continually muddy clothes, rats and no loo will ever go away. I do not want to go back there. It was incredibly kind of David to believe in us and lend us the space – it was only meant to be for a couple of months during the summer, and we were grateful to him for being so generous to me and Toti. I am just saying I would not want to live in an outside yard in a caravan again.

We needed a proper base. We needed somewhere to live for a start, and we needed somewhere to store costumes, to stable horses, to build an office, to build wagons. A circus generates an incredible amount of hardware, all of which needs looking after and storing. Lights, cables, tents, ring boxes, props, costumes, horse harnesses. The little collection of wagons that we had hand-built – the box office, the wardrobe, the four-bunker, our wagon – took a pounding each winter from the ice and snow, and were heartbreakingly worn and peeling. Our costume collection was now stored in our friend Caroline Mann's attic. The tent and the props simply had to just lie out in the yard. Nothing was on hand. Everything was deteriorating. We needed about 2 acres with a building.

We went to see our local MP to ask his advice on what we should do. We explained about the circus and about our problem of where to locate it for its development and future. He said that we should not be living in Gloucestershire, that we must forego the beautiful countryside and relocate to south-west Wales where land was cheaper. I felt confused when he said this. We had both grown up in Gloucestershire. Toti's mum lived here and we did not want to move away from her, and besides, Toti had run a landscaping business here for the last fifteen years. It was really nothing to do with the scenery. It hadn't really occurred to me how beautiful Gloucestershire was – it was just home. I mean, we love it, but we didn't move here seeking nice scenery and country pubs. We grew up here.

We asked the council, who said that we should find some old farm buildings. We asked an estate agent, who said that there were no farm buildings between Cardiff and London that were not occupied. Meanwhile, the wind continued to blow through the yard. We still did not have a bathroom. There was nowhere to make costumes. The tiny box office was the office and the heating system; fan heaters used to keep the harsh blowing wind out meant that it was impossibly hot and stuffy.

Eclipse still stood in a field at the top of the road, disconsolately waiting for something to happen.

At some point around 2002, Toti and I almost gave up. We saw a little terraced house in Cirencester and put in an offer for it. If we had moved there, into the dry and warm, the circus would have been left, I think, in that windswept yard and never picked up again. Then a kind of miracle happened. A man who had bought half of a large isolated farm outside Bourton-on-the-Water made friends with Toti while we were standing at Barrington. He had read on the back of our leaflet that Toti did landscaping. He proposed that Toti could help him work on the farm, sorting out the clogged lakes, streams and rerouting the tracks around the place. The name of the farm was Folly Farm.

The farm had originally been open to the public and had housed a nationally important collection of ducks and geese. The entrepreneurial family had also run a campsite, some lavender fields and a small garden centre and nursery. High on top of the Cotswolds, the land is typical of local sheep pasture, criss-crossed with dry stone walls. It is cold, fairly bleak and windswept. The family sold the farm just after 2000 and the garden centre, nursery and wild-fowl side of the operation had dwindled and closed down. When Toti started work there the duck and geese pens were full of rats and the buildings that had been the nursery and garden centre had fallen into total disrepair – rusty roof trusses, sagging broken insulation, cracked concrete, old seed packet stands abandoned with seed packets still in them and scattering on the wet concrete, an empty cash till, an abandoned charity collecting box in the shape of a small panda, a children's cafe with overturned plastic chairs. Outside, there were rows of abandoned fruit trees fighting for life in small plastic pots, rows of corrugated plastic green houses, and an empty

Above: The Severn Springs yard in winter. (Nell Gifford)

Right: Demolishing and rebuilding Folly Farm. This is Dominic Waldron, the designer, who was a little boy growing up in Minety when we lived there before the accident. (Michael Seadon)

Opposite above: The wagons arriving at Folly Farm. Rebecca Townsend and her boyfriend Duncan Green helping Toti with a tractor. In the foreground is Colin Matthews who sold us the plot. (Nell Gifford)

Opposite below: Toti and me standing in our house after the main shell had been built. (Michael Seadon)

Above: Mending lorries. T.E. Gifford is the engine behind Giffords Circus. (Giffords Circus collection)

children's farmyard, an empty goat stable, some empty chicken pens and, in the field, just one old Jersey cow who had been left behind. Stow-on-the-Wold where the wind blows cold – the next-door village is called Cold Aston and has a second name – Aston Blank. My erudite cousin, who grew up in the village of Hampen, just down the valley, said that this was probably a Norman version of Cold Aston: Aston Blanc. White Cold Aston. Listen to what the ancestors are telling you.

We bought the garden centre plot that sits in the middle of the farm: a Dutch barn and the derelict garden centre, and about an acre or so of ground that had been a nursery, and a car and coach park. I remember arriving at Folly Farm for the first time at the end of the 2002 season and sitting in this grassy area surrounded by high Leylandii evergreen, screening it completely from the road and surrounding area; a secret garden, an outside space that somehow felt inside, finally *our* garden.

The wagons had soon been pulled into the barn, Eclipse was stabled in the old goat pen, where she contently pulled at a hay net strung to an old roof truss, pleased, I think, that her people had finally seen sense and bought her somewhere to live. It was a rough, cold site, populated with rats and broken buildings. There was still no bathroom, or office or anything, but our wagons were under cover in the Dutch barn, safe from the rain and snow and, more than that, it was ours. It was a home. The grass was green and soft; emerald green and soft as silk. The Leylandii tall and protective. The air still. The sun shining. The ground had never felt so firm.

A vast green silk emerald four-poster bed festooned with branches. That was how it felt – a home at last.

What followed was five years of intensive work on Folly Farm to pull it together and create a place that was simultaneously a home and a headquarters. When I look back at these photographs – the smashed buildings, the rubbish-tip ground – I feel grateful for the relatively organised and clean place it is now. But my heart doesn't sink. I don't remember hardship at all, just the immense excitement of building our own place.

The first thing we did was build an office and utility block in the corner of the Dutch barn. By we, I mean Toti. Toti is the best builder in the world, the most practical person you can imagine. He doesn't write much down. It is in his head. To some extent he needs people around him to be able to read his thoughts, for he waits on a project, and then suddenly pounces and in a whirl of breeze blocks, builders, machines and cement mixers, his visions materialise. We then demolished the rest of the buildings. This happened very slowly, because we didn't have a lump of capital to do it all at once, and because we were doing it ourselves, and because we were still touring each year. So the shows were put together amongst the demolition

Above left: Folly Farm, 2003. (Nell Gifford)

Above right: Folly Farm, 2013. (Maria Shickle)

Above left: Rebecca and Ronan, 2003. (Nell Gifford)

Above right: Same girl, same horse, 2013. (Maria Shickle)

work, gold threads weaving in and out of broken breeze blocks, scarred metal and rubbish tips. We started to be able to accept extra work – fashion shoots, a fashion video (starring, yes, me and Rebecca!) and even a pop video. We could put the tent up on the green area, screened by the tall Leylandii, and we became expert at mocking up tent exteriors and interiors amongst the broken buildings – we hung bits of tent walling against breeze-block walls, strung fairy lights, dragged ring boxes across the concrete, scattered sawdust, dressed-out little sets with cases and the old drum and tin horses bought at a Gloucester car-boot sale.

The joy was that, finally, everything was on hand. Costumes, horses and props were all in the same place, and we could assemble and take apart scenes and stages and set-ups at a faster pace. Hence our imaginations could work harder, and be fulfilled quicker. Toti built a little outdoor ring so that Rebecca and I could train young horses. I have learnt that a good facility is absolutely everything; without it you cannot move the show forward. Suddenly, we had a place that was under cover – not exactly warm, and not that dry, but still. We had what was becoming a purpose-built space to play and experiment, try out ideas, make mistakes and have arguments before going on the road.

The demolition took a few years. Toti then built a huge barn for indoor practice and, adjacent to the barn, a house for us to live in. The barn and the house are attached together, and the stables, office and workshop are all inside the barn. This central barn is the engine of our creativity. It is where the imagination plays the hardest and the longest. It is shelter, warmth, light. The big barn seems to hold time in it – the big barn gives us time.

This barn at Folly Farm is, for Toti and me, the fulfilment of so many years of mutual dreaming. It is a fully intergrated space, central to our farm and to our work. It is like a medieval great hall, a shelter and a meeting place.

When you are in the barn each of the departments can watch the other working. The office is on a first-floor mezzanine that overlooks the main training space through a vast internal window. Underneath the office mezzanine are two wardrobe rooms that look out on the main barn space, also through internal windows. It rings with life. It is the engine of the show. Folly Farm is very, very cold. In the winter we are often snowed in for weeks at a time. The place freezes solid and dry, like a weird, cold drought. Then the snow chokes us to a standstill. The roads close. There are slow walks to Cold Aston through deep drifts. The thaw is worse – black, cold mud everywhere. Wet everywhere. The ground slimy, and then weeks and weeks of cold rain on damp snow that sits around, right into the spring. But the barn stays dry and light and we can work on, through dark winter, training, plotting, designing.

The activity in the barn changes with the seasons of the year. It is a flexible space. In the middle of winter it is full of horses, and the very early stages of experimenting with a show. We set up an indoor ring so that we can practise the horses at any

time of day and whatever the weather. For most of the midwinter phase it would be impossible to practise outside. Russian vaulters, a Shetland pony to lie on a sofa, two Hungarian horses enacting the Battle of Borodino. Tweedy and I have spent a whole winter training a young horse to trot in a circle while Tweedy stood on it and juggled. We have experimented with music and aerial acts – Izzy in her hoop, a piper on the bagpipes, Peter Sen on the drums – and auditioned opera singers, the high notes ringing against the steel structure. We have set up snow cannons and enacted the French retreat from Moscow in 1882, we have brought the two vast shire horses inside and Attila, a real Hungarian Csikós rider, rode them around the ring standing up with a foot on each cracking a Hungarian rawhide whip, or *Karakash*, as it is onomatopoeically called in Hungary. But mainly midwinter is a quiet time, patient, low instruction to the horses – brav, stand, walk on – quiet whisperings to trained doves, the sound of the snow falling on the roof of the barn, the fire crackling, the drone of the fan in the chimney,

In the raw early spring, after the thaw, the tent is put up by Toti's landscape team. A cheer rises as the kingpoles go up for the first time in the season, and then a drawn-out period follows as we look at the tent and work out how the interior is going to be. Often there are new elements to work out – sometimes a new tent, or new seats, or a new bandstand (or the old bandstand and old frustrations). It is a world of a cold gravelly yard, ropes, cables and sledge hammers. The soil and sawdust from the main barn is either put in the outdoor ring, or moved into the tent, depending on how compacted it is. New sawdust is put down. Lights and electrics are installed. Heaters are hired locally – the tent is gradually made ready for the horses.

Then the art interns start to arrive. They pitch their tents in the little orchard. Horse practice moves from the main barn to the tent and the barn is swept out and filled with worktops and shelves. Buckets of paint, baskets of fabric scraps and models of the tent are dragged out of dusty storage, and in the office, wardrobe and barn there are long days of drawing, thinking, making mocks, models, threads from props and costumes burning in the fire. The days lengthen and the work intensifies. The musicians arrive, and they practise in Notgrove Village Hall as well as in the barn – saxophones, trombones, violins, harmoniums, accordians, triangles, tympanis. The barn starts to ring with noise and holds a constant motion of people working.

Finally, the full company and the director arrive. More wagons and caravans pour into the farm. The orchard becomes a campsite. The washing machine and drier in the staff utility room run twenty-four hours a day. Our house becomes head office, with production meetings in our kitchen from seven o'clock in the morning, and every available space is taken up with people scheduling, budgeting, writing, sewing, playing, dancing, directing, riding, painting. Vats of tea and coffee are consumed. It is at once a theatre rehearsal, pony club camp, film set, barn dance, farm commune and family. The show is moulded and the tone of the season is set.

This intense spring-time period lasts for three weeks. At the end of it, Toti takes charge of the company and organises the first move out of the farm. It is like an army being mobilised. The company must be at once co-operative and patient, ready to go, and ready to wait. Anything can happen and hold-ups are common. But over the course of a day or so the farm empties, and the barn stands silent again, waiting for our return in September.

Left: The Chandelier Room at Folly Farm. This room is used for display storage and meetings. (Michael Seadon)

MOVING THE CIRCUS

An old friend of ours, a digger driver and groundworker called Colin Cooper, said that when the nuclear bombs go off, and the whole world is covered in fall-out and rubble, you will hear a scraping and a digging sound, and through the rubble will emerge Toti's digger, driven by Toti.

Toti is a groundworker and landscaper who has turned his hand to circus. Art is love.

I like this story because Toti is an unstoppable force of nature. He is determined and practical and, put simply, the circus could not move without him. There is no disaster that stops him, no amount of broken vehicles that will make him despair and give up. He will never give up. He has Herculean strength, is an indomitable leader of men. If Toti Gifford did not exist you would have to invent him – wilder and more magical than any fictional character. Toti can build beautiful barns and houses without any plans. He can move ancient orchards. He has produced a priceless vintage circus from his imagination. Visitors to the circus look at the complex infrastructure of cables and pipes and wagons and tents and generators, all of which gets installed overnight, in a matter of hours, and they can't believe it. They scratch and shake their heads. Toti moves and installs the whole circus without written plans, without hesitation, weekly building a mobile village for sixty people.

These are Toti's pages because this is his work. He designed the tent. He designed the wagons and directed all their construction. He moves the circus and hundreds of trucks, thousands of miles with an ever-changing team of circus performers. He has swept motorways clean of broken glass before the police have time to take off their jackets and help, he has dragged vehicles out of ditches with chains, lifted sunken wagons out of the mud, cheered tired workers into action.

With an iron will, Toti has propelled the circus through the first ten years of touring.

Left: The indomitable Toti digging his way out. (Michael Seadon)

Right: Toti in the summer, front of house. (James Waddell)

Toti's team. Mending, building, driving. (*Left*: Andrew Rees; *clockwise from top left*: Michael Seadon; Michael Seadon; Andrew Rees)

Moving the box office.
(Andrew Rees)

7

MOSCOW TO MINCHINHAMPTON

The Moscow State Circus is a vast institution that covers the whole of Russia. In Moscow itself there are two Moscow State Circus buildings and then there are further buildings for performance and training right across the country. Moscow State Circus artistes join the organisation for life so their training is salaried and they receive a pension upon retiring. They train in the Moscow State Circus buildings and are available for shows at any of the other buildings.

Graham, Toti and I had been talking about doing another trip abroad to find artistes. I have a very old friend, Clem, who was living in Moscow and who spoke fluent Russian. She agreed to help us with some travel plans. Sometime in the winter of 2004 we set off for Moscow. The travel party consisted of me, Graham, Toti and Nancy. We borrowed long fur coats from Toti's mother and, on Clem's advice, bought 'rubber-soled fur-lined walking boots'. We were quite perplexed as to what we should wear. Clem gave advice on footwear, but beyond that she was vague.

'I have not quite cracked it,' she said, 'but it is very cold.'

So we took mountains of polo-necks and cashmere jumpers, also borrowed, and a very strange assortment of fur coats. This meant that we had a lot of luggage. We met Graham at Heathrow, neat and dapper

as ever with a compact travel bag and sports coat.

During our visit to Moscow I wrote an account of visiting a very odd place called the Durov Animal Theatre. It was one of the strangest places I had visited; it really felt like nowhere else I had been before. I didn't really know why we were there as I could not relate any of it to Giffords Circus or see any way to link the two together. I didn't dislike it, I just could not understand it all. This is an account of our visit to the Durov Animal Theatre.

Toti and I set off ahead of Graham and Nancy. It is freezing cold and snowing hard. We take the metro to Svetnoi Boulevard. We walk past the grand Nikulin Circus building. We walk from the boulevard under a giant flyover where we are confronted by a large intersection; eight lanes of fast-moving traffic and a suggestion of a level crossing. The air, which is getting increasingly colder, blows across the open plane of tarmac as if across the Steppe. The sky is thick and heavy with snow, muffling noises. We walk through a park where two larger-than-life dogs cling by their jaws to each other's necks in a static and monumental tug of war. Through the trees and the snow the traffic flickers and drones. We cross through some railings out onto the street, then walk along

Left: Nancy with her camera. She took all the Moscow photographs. (Nancy Trotter)

the gritty scraped pavement to the Durov Animal Theatre.

It is a pale blue-and-white concrete building. On the building are sculptures in strips and barrels of welded steel – an elephant carrying a stick aloft, a bird on each end of the stick, bears on balls, a cockerel. Beside the building, on the edge of a park, we can see two Friesian horses being lunged in a deep outdoor ring, plunging a bit in the loose surface of the ring and the snow. Two huge black horses with curly manes like statues come alive, moving in the cold park through the falling snow like miracles.

We walk around to the staff entrance. We meet up with Nancy and Graham, a security guard and a CCTV system flickering. The guard says something in Russian into a telephone hanging from a paper-strewn wall.

A woman appears through a doorway. She smiles at us kindly and we shake hands. She introduces herself as Marina. She is followed by a man in a smart cord suit, with blue bulging but narrow eyes. He is called Vadim.

We are then ushered off through marble corridors in a strict sequence. They gesture to Nancy, Graham, Toti and me to go first through the doorways, stepping aside and bowing their heads firmly. Toti and Graham then stand aside for me and Nancy. Nancy hesitates and I step forward, followed by Nancy, Graham and then Toti. The gentleman in the cord suit bows his head to Marina, who steps forward followed by Vadim. And thus we proceed around the huge building. It takes some time to get through each of the many doorways, as our little group is joined by other people – a translator, a vet, some more animal trainers – our choreography gaining in complexity with each new person added.

We are led through the corridors of the building, which smell very strongly of animals. In some sections there is a watery reptilian smell, in some an unmistakable smell of hound, in others a more musky smell of herbivore, like deeply rotted straw. At one doorway, as we are poised to organise ourselves to pass through it, the door suddenly swings open and we step back as a tiny old woman in a patterned headscarf, flowery dress, cardigan, ankle socks and flip flops bustles through, carrying a white rat in a cage. In another corridor we are flattened to the wall by a herdsman with three floppy-haired pigs. The man in the corduroy says something to the man with the pigs, who nods and seems to agree. The pigs are unconcerned, snuffling and barging their way along the corridor. We come to a foyer, where families are buying balloons and fizzy drinks, and chatting loudly and happily. We are joined by two other men, also in smart suits, and we all walk towards an office. They stop and gesture to me to walk through the smoked glass-fronted door. I step forward and am followed by Nancy, Graham, Toti, Marina, the vet, a translator, a historian, the two other trainers, and finally followed by the three men in suits. Chairs are pulled up, and I suddenly feel an expectation settle on me to move things forward.

I was feeling a bit overwhelmed by the reception we had received thus far: the appointment was the result of some very vague emails we had exchanged a few months ago. In fact I was wondering, and Toti told me later that he was thinking the same thing, that there must have been some kind of confusion, and that they thought we were someone else.

'We love your building, your work here, and we would like to tell you about our circus in England.' I glanced at Toti and he smiled encouragingly at me. 'We are in the process of starting to put a new show together.'

'Would you like to see our show?' Marina interjected suddenly, beaming. 'Our show in the small theatre. It would be our pleasure to show you.'

Before we can say anything we are all up and off, moving along the curving marble corridors, past some booths selling sweets, past open doors to the left, glimpsing a camel's head blinking lazily at us, a sea lion floating dreamily in a green tank. There is a sound of clucking and crowing and barking and neighing and bellowing. We are then ushered into the back of the theatre. The show is going on – a tabby cat plays hide and seek with a girl in a blue dress, a raven counts on an abacus, a cockerel flutters onto the stage and crows loudly. Pigeons and chickens tug clothes from a clothes line. We watch the show for a while. It is a dramatisation of Russian folk tales and songs using animals as actors, with the trainers – all rosy cheeks and weathered hands – as the supporting cast. It is noisy, slightly chaotic and charming, and the audience laughs and claps with delight.

We are soon ushered out of the little theatre, and are taken back along the corridor, past the stalls, and towards the smoked glass of the office. I expect to resume our meeting, but this is not to be. We pass by the office and bear left, finding ourselves at the foot of a small but very grand marble staircase. The lights are dim and there is dust on the marble. We are taken up the staircase and in the dim watery light we can see plaster of Paris animal shapes on either side, and in a window-sill above the staircase. Neighs and shouts and snorts come dimly through the thick walls, while these statues – antelope, bear, walrus, cockerel, dinosaur, crocodile, hippo, goat – loom dimly. We alight on an elegant circular landing off which lead several heavy wooden doors. We turn and look back down the staircase and on the shelf in front of the window above the stairs a stuffed lion, tiger and bear sit in morbid companionship overlooked by the glassy-eyed bust of a man.

Suddenly, a cross-looking woman with bright red, bobbed hair bursts through one of the doors on the landing, She talks fast and anxiously to Marina, her eyes constantly flicking across to us. She keeps gesturing to the bottom of the stairs. I feel sure that the tour is over. I start to feel that we ought to go. Marina nods, looking very serious. Yes, the tour is over I think. Then Marina turns to us and explains that Elena, the woman with the red hair, is concerned because the tour of the Durov family living quarters starts at the bottom of the staircase, not the top. And as we are all standing at the top of the staircase, on the landing, it is clear that the only solution to this problem is for us to return to the bottom of the staircase and restart the tour.

So we all walk down the stairs and, composure restored, our red-headed guide begins the tour.

'The Durov Animal Theatre was built in 1912 by the great clown and animal trainer Vladimir Durov. Here you will see some of the sculptures he made of his larger animals.' She points to the plaster sculptures. 'Vladimir was the great grandson of Nadezhda Durov, from the old and noble Durov family. She was brave, she was in her way a performer – in 1812 she disguised herself as a man to fight as a cavalry officer against the French. She was a true child of Russia – courageous, and she loved her country so much. Perhaps her eccentricity, her passion, was passed down to her grandsons, for their lives were remarkable too, as we will see. They joined the circus and they became great trainers,

> A tabby cat plays hide and seek with a girl in a blue dress, a raven counts on an abacus, a cockerel flutters onto the stage and crows loudly.

making work that was more beautiful, more experimental and ahead of its time than anything that has come before it.'

We climb the stairs and once again arrive at the little landing, now under the firm guiding hand of Elena. We are all invited to turn at once, to look back down the staircase and, in a manner as if we were being introduced, Elena announces, gesturing to the sculpture of the man under the window, 'and this is Vladimir Durov'.

We then turn and are ushered, re-forming our proper sequence, through one of the heavy doors that lead off from our little landing. The room we enter is furnished with dark wooden furniture, fine examples of the Russian Empire style; tub chairs, embroidered screens, polished wood set off by mounts of gilded wood and bronze, borrowing motifs from ancient art. There is a large heavy table in the middle of the room and a little sitting room leading off to one side. On the walls are lurid Russian landscape paint-

ings, faded black-and-white photographs of formal-looking men, glamorous women and, of course, animals – every species, in paintings, sculpture and photographs.

'These are the private rooms of Vladimir Durov,' Elena begins. 'They have not been touched since he died. In here he would entertain many friends, illustrious friends, actors, politicians. He developed his own system of training, quite different from anything else, and his methods and the things he discovered are still practised today at the Durov Animal Theatre. No trainer here uses a whip but rather we investigate the natural behaviour of the animal and it is that which we use in our training methods. Durov's work contributed significantly to the understanding of animal behaviours.

'Yes,' she said, very seriously, 'While Durov enjoyed the highlife of show business, research into animal behaviours and psychology of the most serious kind was carried out here.'

I stared at the wall and at the face of the Durov dynasty. I thought about Toti and Giffords Circus and I wondered if, one day, there would be a tour of a building somewhere by our relatives and whether all the work we did would be ongoing, cherished and kept so carefully by unknown future people. The Russians stand quietly while we look at the paintings and the furniture. Through the glass of the windows snow falls and it is getting dark, creating a muffled and cosy atmosphere inside the room. I wished at that precise moment that everyone I knew and loved – Mum, Rick, Clover, Emma, Tom, Sophy, Teesa; everyone – was there with me. Sometimes the circus feels like a bringing home of emotion.

We go on and on into the museum. It becomes more and more strange, a dark place behind a mirror, a place that you visit in a dream, familiar, vivid and secret. It is warm and quiet. All of Durov's animals are displayed, preserved by taxidermy, behind glass. There is a group of animals sitting around a table having tea – pigs, goats, cats, foxes, ferrets. There is a beautiful black carriage pulled by a dog and another carriage pulled by a furry pig. There is a train set, about half the size of a full-size train, in which sit a group of monkeys. Hawks and eagles hover in dark corners, everywhere there are photographs, books, paintings, cabinets of toys sent to the theatre by their devoted patrons.

We are then led through the museum, past reindeer and kindly owls, and tabby cats and old dogs to a wall where hang two dark blue velvet curtains. Somebody behind the scenes must have been watching us. Somebody unseen. For an imperceptible hand dims the lights and, as if by magic, the curtains draw back and a model train set is revealed, set back into the wall. At that moment a train comes out from the wall, through a tunnel, and trundles around the track and stops at a model station. The door of the station opens and six plump white mice run out, jump off the train and set off around the track.

'Now the mice will journey north into the snow.'

The lights within this little theatre dim and the surrounding landscape through which this miniature train runs starts to glow, like stars lit by snow, like a snowy landscape seen from the windows of the Trans-Siberian express on a cold night as you rush further and further away from your home, your travelling companions like white mice. The blue curtain swishes shut, the dim lights come back up, and we are guided back through the museum and back out onto the little landing.

That was the end of the Durov visit. If you visit Moscow, go and check it out.

Nancy and I were struggling somewhat with our wardrobe decisions. Moscow is so vast and impenetrable. At the end of every day you feel full of black soot and grease, as if you have been working on an oil rig in the Arctic Ocean. Walking is hard because it is so icy, made harder still by heavy shoes and layers and layers of cashmere and fur. The temperature inside the buildings is boiling hot, it is as hot inside as it is cold outside, only everyone forgot to mention this, and so a lot of time is taken is up with the removal of clothes and then the endless dressing before heading out again. Anyone who says to wear layers is wrong – you end up sweaty and tired, endlessly pulling off jumpers and t-shirts until you are exhausted. Nancy and I swapped boots, borrowed jumpers and tramped the streets behind my old friend Clem; I found myself wishing I was wearing a swimming costume covered by a floor-length hooded mink coat, which, and now I understand why, was a pretty standard evening outfit for the racy Russian girls.

Right: Moscow streets – Toti and Clem. (Nancy Trotter)

Clem took us to her hangouts, restaurants and bars, where she met her circle of literary expats and Russians. Our reason for being there, that we were looking for circus artistes, was met with some puzzlement and even a little dismissal. The circus was by no means fashionable or current in Russian literary circles, as it had become in England. We drank vodka and munched on delicious bowls of herbs in a restaurant specialising in Armenian food.

But we had to find some artistes.

We visited the Great Moscow Circus, a state-owned circus building located at the Vernadsky Prospekt. This building, built in 1971, was one of over seventy circus buildings in the Soviet states that were at that time controlled under the Soviet Union. Thousands of performers worked for this circus organisation and although salaries were not high in comparison to western equivalents, employment was secure, there was the opportunity to develop within a specialist training school system, and equipment, accommodation and travel was provided.

Moscow, huge and implacable, frozen solid and snowing, men wrapped like mummies slowly chipping ice off the pavements all day long. Cold that seems to bore through your body to your bones. You cannot stand still. If you stand still you feel as if you are going to die. Packs of stray dogs that lie on the grills above the metro and then run down the escalators into the warmth of the stations and move around the city on trains.

Out of the metro we crossed a snowy desert tundra of ring roads to reach a bare-boned park, across which we could see the giant concrete flying saucer of the circus building. A beautiful woman with two giant Borzoi hurried past. Street vendors were selling pancakes and, curiously, ice cream, just their eyes visible, the rest of their bodies padded and wrapped against

Above: Outside the Vernadsky Prospekt Moscow State Circus building. (Nancy Trotter)

the cold. We saw a huge billboard showing two blonde-haired body builders and lions leaping through hoops of fire. We found our way to the back of the giant building. There were electric doors and a security man at a desk. Toti and I went forward with our little Giffords Circus programmes, but the security man shook his head and closed his eyes. People were streaming in and out through the security gates. To us they were closed. We retreated back out onto the edge of the park. We didn't know what to do. Our stammered Russian words were getting us nowhere.

Then it happened. As we were conferring, one of the two blonde-haired body builders from the poster walked past on his way into the building. In a flash, Graham followed him and politely caught his attention. He held his hand out, and said his family and stage name – Graham Chipperfield. An expression of recognition, surprise and delight spread over the blonde boy's face.

'Chipperfield? Really? Nice to see you! Hello! I am Edgard Zapashny.'

He shook Graham's hand and hugged him warmly. It was like Graham was his long-lost brother. He spoke to Graham in fluent, heavily accented, English. He asked him about his family, how his brother was, and when he asked him what he was doing in Moscow, Graham indicated towards us and introduced us and communicated that we were here to learn more about the Russian circus scene.

'Can we come in do you think?'

Edgard laughed.

'Of course, of course, come with me, anyway. Come on, it is cold out here. Come on, this way.'

With a wave of his hand and a nod from the guard we were through the doors and into the building.

'Anyway, look I have to go, my friend, we have to practise. But good to see you and if you want to watch us practise it is through there. If you want to see a show it's best to ask in the office, right there. It's Irina who does the tickets for guests – I will tell her you are here later and you will be fine. See you around, my friends.'

With that, he was off.

Green corridors, concrete, harsh lighting. The building was very warm. Clem told us that free heating was a left-over perk from the Communist system. We went right and then left down a corridor, past dressing rooms with doors left ajar – where we could see people sitting at dressing tables, piles of DVDs, wires, computers, discussions, tantalising glimpses into the artistes' lives – past offices and more corridors leading off into indoor stabling. We then went through a wide entrance past piles of huge crash mats into a vast training space. It was a full-size training ring with balconies surrounding it on two floors. The floor around the ring was oak parquet. The ring itself was painted on the outside with chipped brown gloss paint and there were two rows of battered leather tip-back chairs full of viewers. The light washed over everything with a kind of lemon hum and there were no shadows. The ring boxes were wide and heavy, and the ring itself close-carpeted in coconut matting. There were hundreds of rigging points in the walls and in the ring. It was very quiet except for the occasional voices of the performers training. There were mirrors all around. A tall, thin man stood outside of the ring in front of a mirror juggling handfuls of clubs. He stayed there all the time. A girl was doing a series of back somersaults on the feet of an older acrobat who was upside down in a kind of flat chair, while a trainer counted in Russian – *odeen, dva, tree, chetree, pyet, shest, sem, vosem*. We sat down in the red seats, took off our coats and piled up our bags behind the seats. People walked by us and sometimes looked at us and nodded, but mainly we were invisible.

The training continued throughout the day, relentless, mechanical, focused, unselfconscious. We watched a man teaching a group of white cats to jump through a series of hoops along the ring fence. There was a rearranging of the ring surface and a procession of wiry tall horses were led in, along with the arrival of some men who started practising on the horses, classic Russian Cossack riding. Later there were more gymnasts. It was hours of pure, uncut circus material.

At some point later in the day, the two blonde tamers reappeared and asked Graham if we would like to see through into the main ring. We followed them out of the practice area down through another wide corridor and out into the main performance ring. This was a vast auditorium. It probably seated upward of 3,000 people. It was an indoor circus on an industrial scale, and is thought to be the biggest stationary circus in the world, to date. The ring that we could see, at that moment set up for the imminent practice of the Zapashny brothers with their horses and their lions, was in fact just one of a series of arenas, all stacked on top of each other like a vast pile of napkin rings or hoops. Each arena served a different purpose – equestrian, water, illusionist, ice rink, light-effect – and these rings could be swapped during a performance by being raised or lowered using an underground mechanised system. At one point we were shown down underneath the building where we observed oily workers cranking huge handles to move the rings about.

We sat in the main space and watched the two blonde brothers tear about the ring at an incredible speed, juggling fire from the back of two huge cart horses. We watched them with their lions, and at one point one of the two brothers sat astride a lion as it jumped through a blazing fire hoop. We spent the rest of that day watching the artistes working in the back practice ring, honing their

skills to perfection. Toti fell asleep behind the seats. We were completely undisturbed by anyone in the building. We were the invisible people.

At one point we were thinking that we might head back to the hotel. We had seen lots of performers but none that looked quite right for our show and, being invisible, the thought of actually approaching anyone and offering them a job in England seemed a daunting prospect. We were so close, and yet so far. We had come to Moscow to find an act, and time was running out. It was Graham who told us not to leave. He pointed out that we had come to find acts, and that we were sitting in the biggest Russian State Circus building in Russia, we did not know who we would see next. He was right. We settled back into our red leather seats and continued watching. The artistes came and went. The air was hot. The juggler was still working in front of the mirror, moving his clubs rhythmically. Trolleys of animal feed were wheeled past.

Then, late into the afternoon, three men started to practise an act. They had a long springy bar, a man situated at either end, while they flipped the third man into the air from the bar.

'This looks quite good,' said Graham, settling back and folding his arms. 'It would work in your tent.'

We watched the men. The flier – the man who springs from the bar – was neat, short and had a soft, clean face framed with short hair. He had a calm, neutral expression. There was a man with a moustache who seemed to be quite angry with the second catcher, a man with a red face, permanent frown and thick black hair. We had the impression that the moustached man and the flier were instructing him, and were angry with him for not picking it up quicker. We all felt quite nervous of the moustached man. He seemed quite furious. The red-faced second catcher did not

Left top: The Zapashny brothers working. (Nancy Trotter)

Left bottom: A trained cat. (Nancy Trotter)

say anything at all. We watched them practising for a time, for about an hour or so.

'It looks like they are winding up, no?' asked Graham. 'Go and talk to them,' he encouraged.

The red-faced second catcher was now sitting on the ring fence breathing hard. The moustached man was talking animatedly to the little calm flier, one hand in his pocket, the other hand gesticulating. The little flier listened and twitched his nose, his eyes flicking about the room.

I suddenly felt nervous, as if I couldn't move. I had one of our programmes from the year before in my hand, ready to show them.

'Go on.'

I looked at Toti. He slowly leant forward and then stood up. I handed him the programme and he took it in both hands and held it in front of him, as you might carry a prayer book. He coughed. He looked nervous too.

Slowly, Toti and I walked toward the ring and around the outside of it until we were as close to the three men as we could be without actually climbing into the ring, which we would not have done uninvited. They noticed that we were trying to approach them and the tall moustached man and the little flier came over to us.

'Hello. Sorry, no Russian,' we said.

They looked at us and, to my amazement, they smiled warmly and politely and nodded.

'It's OK, no problem, we have a little English.'

Toti ploughed on.

'We have a little circus in England. We see you. We like this act. Maybe we can talk about working.'

And with that faltering, nervous introduction, we were in. What followed was a series of meetings in Moscow. The moustached man was called Sasha and was a poet,

gentle and clever. When we met somewhere in town a day later to discuss the contract and what would happen, he seemed above all concerned that Toti was not wearing a warm hat. He said that the Russian cold will break you, like a twig. I remember that clearly, crossing a road in the cold and the snow, and his metaphor – break like a twig. The flier was called Uri Slipchenko. He was neat and discreet. He pursed his lips when he smiled and his eyes twinkled when he talked. They were both kind and charming to spend time with. They were willing to come to England and they advised us to go back to the circus building and organise their contracts through the circus administration, which we did. The third man, the red-faced catcher, was, they explained, a new partner called Igor and they were teaching him the act. They said they liked him and that he would be good.

It was strange. They seemed so different to how they had been when we were watching them. But this is something I have learnt about Russians: it often looks as if they are having a huge row, but they are not. It is their way.

He said that the Russian cold will break you, like a twig. I remember that clearly.

We met again in a hotel and signed contracts. The next time we would see them would be in England.

The Trio Slipchenko were, as it turned out, brilliant to work with. They were collaborative and open to direction. We dressed them as ring boys, which for many circus artistes is unacceptable as it implies a lack of status, but they happily accepted this idea and understood that it served a story line – they were to play ring boys until the end of the show so that their three-man gymnastic act would be an explosive surprise.

Sasha brought his 12-year-old son with him to England and on days off took him to Stratford to see Royal Shakespeare Company productions. He seemed to be

determined to teach his son as much as possible about England and about circus. He got on very well with Tweedy, who again and again remarked on Sasha's incredible ring craft and subtlety.

Uri brought his wife Natalia and his little boy Ivan, who used to peer through the caravan curtains watching people coming and going. We occasionally lent Uri and Natalia our car and they would, before using it to go on an outing, completely deep clean it. They were like that – very tidy, very clean, meticulously well organised and private.

The third man, Igor, made friends with that year's stable crew and had a fine old time of it, I think, doing the rounds of Cotswold pubs and parties.

At the end of the season they all went home. We had spoken to Uri and Sasha about returning the following season. They seemed keen, although Sasha was tired and had opted out of the finale for the last week or so of the season.

In the winter, around New Year, we received a fax from Uri. It said that Sasha had died over the winter.

We were completely shocked. It did not seem possible. We thought back to Sasha, about his remark about the twig, and his careful time with his son. Toti and I suspected that he knew he was ill when he came, that the circus was a last trip for him and his son, and his last work with his friend and long-time colleague Uri.

We held a little memorial service for Sasha. We planted an oak tree in the garden at Folly Farm. Gerald said that, for him, Sasha was not dead, and in a way I agreed. He was still in Moscow, in the snow, a Russian poet. Maybe that is also to do with the circus, and the way it works. You make very close friends with people each year, and then they go away, a long way away, and often you will never see them again. But somehow they are still there, and still with you – truly a global community.

A WORLD WITHOUT HORSES IS NO WORLD FOR THE CIRCUS

If there ever came a time when we could not for some reason have horses in our show then we would not do a show at all. For me, they are absolutely the core of what we do. A horse makes the occasion. They have an innate theatricality that I find endlessly interesting. I would travel to the ends of the earth to see a horse-based show. A show worth making a pilgrimage to.

The horses have been a constant source of inspiration for the shows. The grey mare and the ballerina on horseback, the black stallion in The Pearl, the fiery red chestnut ponies in The Cockerel Show, the cart horses and the Csikós horse in Caravan. The shows are sculpted around the horses and I am reacting to their colours, their characters, their natures, their stage presence and their historical precedents.

The horses give of themselves with generosity. We have to be very careful not to take too much. The horses' welfare is paramount. Our horses are owned by us and they are trained at Folly Farm. They are looked after by a team of people that include a dentist, a farrier, a chiropractor, a vet, a yard manager and a head trainer. They are ridden out and have regular turnout in big paddocks. Many of the show horses are turned out for the winter, and do not come in, unless the weather is exceptionally bad. They grow shaggy coats, roll in the mud and return to a semi-feral state. I think that this is important for them both mentally and physically.

Sometimes we sell our horses to approved homes, and we have found that they often go on to make good horses for Riding for the Disabled, or as therapy horses. The black-and-white cob from Caravan went to a place called The Fortune Centre that works with disabled adults.

Left: Full House, our Shire horse. (Andrew Rees)

Right: Eclipse. (Olga Sienko)

He is their Christmas carol service pony, his year of working with a live band serving him well – he will stand quietly in a church. The Csikós pony from Caravan went to a Pony Club home, while Eclipse's offspring have been sold on as riding horses.

There are some that never go – Eclipse, of course, and Red, and the shires. They have proved themselves to be entirely suitable for this work, relaxed in the ring and versatile enough to be a dressage horse one season and a vaulting horse the next. These old timers stroll through the season. They go calmly on and off the lorry, calmly into their stables each week. They know their routines. They ignore the music. They tell us through their gait and demeanour if the drums are a bit too loud for them, for example, and we adjust the music accordingly. I am quite sure that they know when we are near the end of a season, when the nights draw in and the ground is dark and the grass is dewy, and I am sure that they look forward to the autumn turn-out and rest.

These horses are not cruelly treated and they are not neglected. They are kept in

Below: Emily Campbell on Mappo. (Andrew Rees)

peak condition and their needs are met. They come first. Their training is careful and methodical. We as trainers go into the training space with a reverence for the process and for the horse – we must impress them. I have learnt techniques for lowering my own heart beat and adrenaline levels in training – raised heart beat and pumping adrenaline do not help human or horse. Careful repetition, praise, the elimination of anxiety – these are just a few principles of horse training. We must go in carefully, we must not be tired, or hungover, or in a rush. The training process is to be respected and its disciplines and protocols adhered to, because at that moment, as you train, either as humans or as humans and horses together, you are doing something that is the most important thing in the world. You must keep your eye on what you are doing unflinchingly and without compromise. For me, our circus and our work with horses is quite the opposite of cruel – it is a joyful ritual, where horse and rider are complicit, a ritual that honours and celebrates the horse.

Below left: Two Giffords Circus treasures – Rob Mann and Red. (Andrew Rees)

Below right: Me on Red. (Andrew Rees)

Left: Rooster.
(Giffords Circus
collection)

Above: Tamerlan on
Rooster. (Giffords
Circus collection)

Right: Tweedy on
Dominoe. (Giffords
Circus collection)

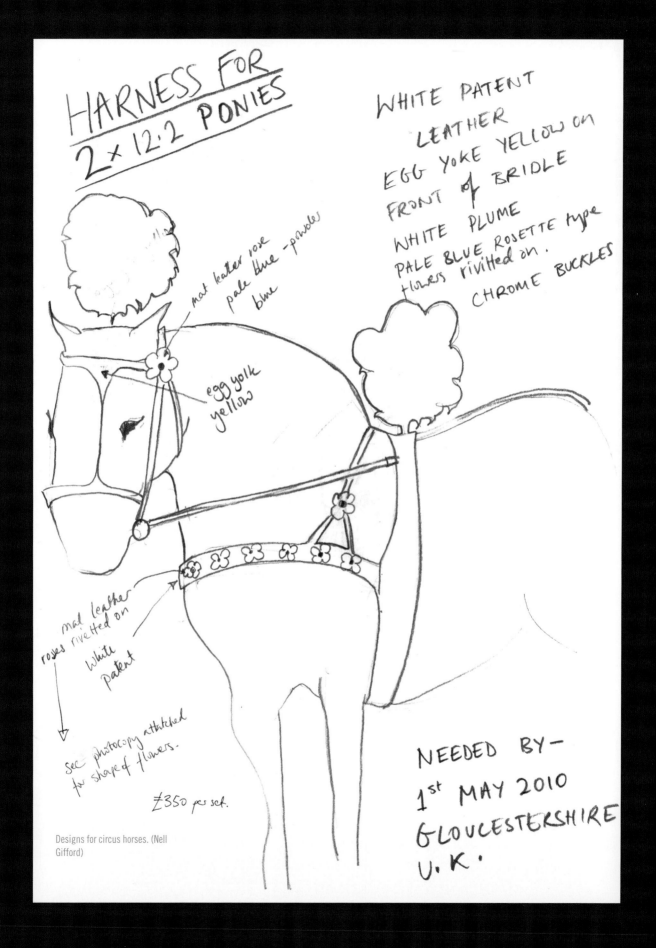

HARNESS FOR
2 × 12·2 PONIES

WHITE PATENT
LEATHER
EGG YOKE YELLOW on
FRONT of BRIDLE
WHITE PLUME
PALE BLUE ROSETTE type
flowers rivitted on.
CHROME BUCKLES

mat leather rose
pale blue - powder
blue

egg yolk
yellow

Mat leather
roses rivetted on
white
patent

See photocopy attached
for shape of flowers.

£350 per set.

Designs for circus horses. (Nell
Gifford)

NEEDED BY –
1st MAY 2010
GLOUCESTERSHIRE
U.K.

Me on Eclipse.
(Giffords Circus
collection)

Left: Me on Perlo. (Giffords
Circus collection)

Above left: Red. (Giffords
Circus collection)

Above right: Tamerlan
riding Rooster and Red.
(Giffords Circus collection)

Early morning on Cheltenham Racecourse! Me on Red, Toti on Full House and professional jockey Tony Evans on Dominoe – at least someone knew where they were going! (Giffords Circus collection)

Eclipse. (Giffords Circus collection)

Ruslan and Red.
(Giffords Circus
collection)

8

COSSACKS IN THE COTSWOLDS

By the end of the 2004 season I was having my doubts about Miriam, the barefooted tiny Dutch woman with the lilting accent, and Roger, her English boyfriend. I started to look elsewhere for horse trainers. The public loved the sight of Miriam – festooned with tiny gold coins, pattering around the ring with her massive black stallion – and Roger – a fairly creditable toreador in his Spanish rider's outfit astride a cream Andalusian horse. But they had become a dark presence on the circus ground. Their large Rottweiler menaced the air in the stables, and they withdrew from the company. At each new ground they would hang tarpaulins and bird cages around their caravans to screen themselves off from everyone else. It was no surprise when, at the end of the season, they vanished in the night, leaving a pile of horse manure and an empty tack room.

An advert in *Horse and Hound* to replace them prompted a reply from a stranger who would become a friend, and altered the whole course of Giffords Circus, maybe forever. I didn't know it then but we were about to make a giant shift as a company; my perspective was about to change, my perception of who we were and what we could achieve artistically to be challenged to a degree that nothing would ever be the same again.

Somebody who signed themselves as Olga in firm, intelligent handwriting sent me a red blurry photograph of a Cossack galloping at an angle around a circus ring. On the back was a message, 'We have good riders, good horses. We can train some good horses for your show', followed by a London phone number.

Olga turned out to be a Polish lady who lived in a vast warehouse near Borough Market and kept six large Borzoi dogs on the roof. She appeared as a kind of twenty-first-century dilettante of everything exotic. She told me about a man and his family who ran the shop at the corner of her street in order to fund a world of race horses and racing dogs in Afghanistan. Olga trod a dangerous, romantic path; she had a kind of innocent love for this stranger at the end of the street and his life back home, which might be violent, or might be mundane, but just might be something more beautiful than you could have imagined. She was mournful and sad, but the coin always fell the right way with her dealings with people as she took those strangers to her heart and lived through them, and thus a kind of alchemy happened around her strange, vague world. She wore steel glasses and fluttering clothes and drove through London like an explorer in her green van.

Olga had befriended some Cossack dancers who were working on a Cossack dance show. She became, as is her way, their friend and ambassador in London, inviting them to her urban mansion where, high in the beams of her warehouse, they feasted together on dried fruits and sushi, drank vodka and with absolute sincerity toasted her Cossack heart as she became their friend.

The heart of the Cossack knows a dog-eat-dog world. These men were not actually Cossacks, but came from deeper in Russia, further south than the Don and the lands of the Cossack; they were from the Caucasus, Dzigits – a rural, patriarchal, martial caste of people who passed down their traditions of horsemanship and fighting from generation to generation. They were in love with their violent, beautiful mountains, where it was a struggle to stay alive in a world of hard drinking, guns and a constant jostling for position and political sway over the man beside you. And yet bashfully, they admitted a genuine friendship with Olga – she was their friend, a good woman, and they liked her. And in return she loved them. She adored their chivalrous, courtly ways, their elaborate good manners, their rituals and convictions. They were from North Ossetia – Alans, who were convinced that they shared their genes with King Arthur, their hero. Olga's theory was that they share with us a Celtic origin, that the Celts journeyed from Central Asia and settled on the Caucasian mountains as well as travelling further to Britain.

A rural, patriarchal martial caste of people, who passed down their traditions of horsemanship and fighting generation to generation.

'Look at the symbols the Ossetians use in their metal work, it is the same as the Celtic metal work you see here – the animal with the face turning backwards, that is uniquely Celtic and Ossetian in origin,' she later told me.

It turned out that we were to work with these people for several years, and there did seem to be an uncanny familiarity

about them, a shared sense of humour, of the absurd, an eye contact that maybe did reach over barriers of time, geography and language. We connected in a way that was to do with a shared identity, and when the circus stopped for a week on the banks of the Severn, on the fields of the Lydney Park Estate, I discovered that Lydney is one of this country's most important Celtic burial sites. There we were camped with these dark-eyed men who by night strolled the hedgerows innocently poaching rabbits and pheasants for the barbeque. It did seem like a strange collision of historical fact and conjecture … but then that is the circus: a coming together of different cultures and peoples that can seem almost biblical, pre-ordained. The circus season – with its extremes of tiredness, and its exclusion of any communication other than directly between people in a rough and muddy field, in advance stages of exhaustion, delirium and excitement – can lead to all sorts of epic speculation. The fact was, we all loved the Cossacks, and it worked well for them to at least give us the impression that the feeling was mutual. Never try to guess what a Russian is thinking, let alone an Ossetian.

The night I met Olga in London, the Thames gliding past below the high windows of her house, Olga introduced the Cossacks to me. Tamerlan, with his mouth set more serious than his close-set eyes, and Elena, his silently judgemental pretty Siberian wife with a blonde-haired, tough-looking baby gazing out from the same close-set eyes, and Ibeer, blue-eyed, square-jawed, shy

Right: My mood board in our living wagon. (James Waddell)

and handsome. We did a deal. Olga translated and Tamerlan, Toti and I made eye contact, swapped smiles. There was a lot of hand-to-heart gesturing, some dispute over fees, poring over photographs, some fuzzy footage on a DVD of a horse galloping in a circus ring. Tamerlan Berezov would come to England just after Christmas with two other Cossacks, Dzigits, it was agreed. He would bring some saddles, bridles and costumes, and he would train two horses, which we would buy, to do two acts for our circus. In one act he would stand up on two horses at once. In the other act they would do jumping, that is, Cossack tricks like riding backwards, hanging off the side of the horse and so on. We paced around one of the large empty rooms in Olga's house to show the size of our ring. Tamerlan said that it was a small ring, smaller than normal, but that he could work in this space, he was quite sure. We agreed a fee for training, a fee for the season, we shook on it, and the deal was done.

It seemed improbable, back at Folly Farm, that three Caucasian horsemen who the public would recognise as Cossacks, but who we now knew were in fact Dzigits, were going to come and live with us in our barns and caravans, and train some horses that we would buy. What had seemed logical in Olga's great echoing warehouse rooms seemed suddenly full of traps and problems. What kind of horses, exactly, would we buy? How would we speak to each other, given we had no language in common? There were critical voices, some real and some imagined, running through my head. It was dangerous, too difficult. The barriers of language and culture were insurmountable. A close friend and wild animal trainer said firmly that it would not work, that it had been tried before but that it failed – the Cossacks needed their own breed of horses. But floating above the Thames we

had done a deal with Tamerlan and, even though he was now thousands of miles away in his home village in North Ossetia, it was a matter of honour to fulfil this contract. There was no going back.

Tamerlan had told us that he needed two horses of about 15 hands. They had to be stallions or at least geldings, but definitely not mares. They must be a solid dark colour and they must be around 5 years old. He said he would train them in three months.

We considered buying some thoroughbreds from the sales, but our circus ring is only 27 feet across and a thoroughbred's stride is long and straight. We needed something that would be agile, that could turn fast and keep its balance on a small circle. We also needed two horses of the same height, because Tamerlan was planning to ride two at once, a foot on each.

On Boxing Day 2004 Toti and I drove to Lincolnshire, on the advice of my aunt, Theresa, to look at two chestnut Welsh cobs, a matched pair. We drove north up the Fosse Way. The roads were empty, the pubs and houses bright, the radio full of songs. It was dark by the time we got there and so we had to look at them lit only by one flood light in an outdoor school. The two ponies stood side by side, obedient and quiet, and then a girl rode them around. Toti and I crouched down at the edge of the school, imaging what they would look like in the circus ring. They flashed red and flaxen and their necks arched. They were small and compact and could turn and bend. Furthermore, the Welsh blood gave them a fiery, wild presence. They were perfect and so we bought them.

I called the ponies Red and Rooster. The new show was to be called The Cockerel and these two red ponies embodied what I hoped would be its macho, red and gold exuberant spirit. This is how a show forms, in impressions, semantics, colours, images, a whirl of papers, designs and

Drawings towards the show. (Nell Gifford)

scripts, with a horse standing squarely in the middle.

The voices kept saying to me: 'It won't work. It never does. Those Cossacks need their own horses.'

'It is taking too big a risk. They won't be able to train them in time.'

But, so what? We were in too deep by that time. The men were under contract. I had struggled through the complex work permit and visa applications, and succeeded. In good faith, in North Ossetia, Tamerlan, his wife Elena, baby, and his two friends had packed six months' worth of clothes, saddles, bridles, whips, knives and animal-hide costumes. Our futures and their futures were becoming more and more bound up together and to back out now was unthinkable, would be a disgrace – we had to honour the deal, as did they, and their arrival was imminent.

A week or so before they were due to arrive some very old friends came to visit. Chris had been working in Spain on the coast, and his brother Oliver had come down to meet him from Shropshire. There are some friends whose arrival is an event – work stops, the fattened cow is killed. One wild night in the pub, jukebox turned up, tables pushed back, the hour turning on itself again and again until we fell asleep where we landed, in chairs around the fire and under the carpet. The next morning I went for a ride with Oliver, on the new ponies, and we set off across the field. However, my pony bucked causing me to half fall, half jump off, twisting my ankle beneath me. I got back on but pain was shooting up my leg, so I carefully slipped off again and sat down knowing that I couldn't walk. Stupidly, with a sinking heart sitting in the wet grass, I realised that I had broken my leg. The timing could not have been worse, and I had only myself to blame. We were only three months away from the start of rehearsals. Rehearsals! Where I have to

be in three places at once, ride four times a day, climb ladders, jump in and out of the ring, walk up and down the seats; stand, walk, run, dance, all day, non-stop for four weeks, followed by the tour – roads, fields, parades, show after show until your body is so tired you can't stand and you have lost 2 stone in weight because a circus season is a machine of relentless and repetitive activity. And there I was, with a snapped ankle, unable to train or ride or even walk, with Dzigit strangers about to arrive at the yard.

In some ways that broken ankle was a blessing, though for sure it did not feel like one. As I arrived back from the hospital on crutches with my leg in plaster and slowly and painfully climbed the wet and slippery steps into the wagon, I realised, as sharp pains ran up and down my leg with every movement, that the four walls of that stuffy little space were going to be pretty much it for six weeks. I sat down on the sofa and, resolving to turn misfortune to fortune, picked up a piece of costume for the forthcoming show and started to embroider. Scraps of fabric, broken jewellery, sequins, stones, metal work, ribbons, ornaments: I covered that costume and then another, and then a saddle cloth and then some more costumes as they arrived back from the makers. It was a blessing because I had nothing else to do but sit in our hot caravan thinking, drawing, reading, sewing. I couldn't go outside and train Eclipse, I couldn't go to London for meetings. I couldn't go for site meetings or planning meetings of any sort, I just had to sit and dream up the show. Embroidery. Drawings. More embroidery.

I stared at the photographs that I had of the Cossacks and wondered what they would be like to live with, how things would go on the yard. I was infused with the colours of the Cossacks that seemed to come from that first photograph – red, yellow, gold – and the idiom for the show was their

Right: Nancy and I designing The Cockerel Show. (Nell Gifford; Nancy Trotter)

152

The jewel of the carnival.

heavily decorated with BS mix? naturally.

unbridled, codified masculinity, their sense of themselves as riders and warriors. This project, the training of the horses, had to work – the show depended on it. I knew that I had to forge a strong relationship with Tamerlan. The troupe was his – Troupe Tamerlan – and the two men that he was bringing with him were essentially sub-contractors. The two men would answer to Tamerlan, and he would answer to me and Toti. Or he would look after his men and we would look after him. Or, to look at it another way, the men were his responsibility – he would need to motivate them, direct them, organise them – and we in turn would be directing him. The wild thing about Tamerlan Berezov is that he was a breakaway from a bigger Moscow-based Russian troupe, called the Kantemirov Troupe. This large group of Russian male stunt riders tours the world as a Cossack act under Kantemirov's iron rule. They live a life of constant shows, but in a way, and more importantly, a life of contsant training. Training, training, training. Tamerlan had made a wild move by leaving the troupe in a kind of renegade manner, and, as we were to find out, he had little or no experience in management. With only the most threadbare resources, he had set up his own troupe. Giffords Circus was his first client.

The hours passed. More embroidery, more drawings, more embroidery.

The arrival of the boys was imminent, and so we made plans. Two cars would go to Heathrow, one for the Tamerlan, his wife Elena, their baby and Tamerlan's troupe, Dagir and Albert, and another car, a pick-up, for all their saddles and equipment. Toti and I prepared the caravans for the Cossacks. We were providing them with very basic touring caravans to live in. We tried to make these caravans as welcoming as possible and my notes from that time reveal these efforts:

Left: The jewel of the carnival. (Nell Gifford)

Cossacks – welcome greeting and things for caravans
- Map (local area)
- List of post office, vet, garage, supermarket, doctor
- Loaf of bread, milk, cups, teaspoons, flowers, programmes, bottle of wine

In that strange time of waiting I also bought a 'teach yourself Russian' system. This is what I am talking about, that there was a turning point for me by the signing up of this little troupe. Until then I had made no real effort to learn the languages that I had been coming into contact with. Yes, I could swear in Hungarian, and say the odd word in German, but essentially I had assumed, having been taught French in the dry, corrective manner typical of England, where the theory of grammar has to be mastered before you can for a moment touch the fun of learning languages, that I was not capable of learning a language. But I was worried about how I would get on with Tamerlan, and I suddenly saw that a small amount of Russian on my side, rather than just leaning on his English, might help.

The day came and Toti and one other driver went to London to meet them. The troupe arrived at the yard and they looked stranger than they had in London. I remember very clearly the first time I saw them at Folly Farm. It was in the big rehearsal barn, where the concrete floor is well trodden and cleanly swept, where the silver winter light palely feeds down from the sky lights. There is a huge fireplace at one end, stained black from smoke – the domain of outdoor cats, Toti's dogs and the boys when they get back cold from work, and hang about by the fire smoking and drinking cider. The stables are adjacent to the barn, and at that moment we had set up a circus ring in the centre of the barn, which was lit by overhead flood lights. The ring glowed silently and the ponies rustled in their boxes. Three

short men appeared from the door that leads from the barn through the workshop to the caravans. They looked vulnerable in the way that people do when they have just got off a plane. They wore their smartest clothes with their bags, their expectations and their worry, dread and excitement written right across them. Tamerlan was first to say hello, and he had a jovial, laughing, direct look in his close-set eyes and a very strong handshake. He is quite short – about 5 foot 6 or 7 – I always feel very tall around him, as in the company of jockeys. He introduced me to a stout, 30-something man with pursed pouting lips and serious eyes; he looked like a banker. This was Dagir. I think my first shy attempts to speak Russian to them were met with total incomprehension. He then introduced me to an older man, Albert. Albert had Asiatic features, a moustache and spoke no English at all. Dagir and Albert. They wore dark suits and long pointy-toed shoes.

After that initial greeting we had welcome drinks in my caravan. Tamerlan was serious, articulate and communicated very well in good English. Albert's wide face was like alabaster. He didn't seem to be looking at anyone. Dagir was silent, bright-eyed and suddenly became very animated and cheerful, which seemed to come from nowhere, changing my impression of him from a kind of calculating hard man to a noisy bon viveur. They seemed to want to formalise the little meeting we were having, which we did by toasting our future project together. I felt that things were going well. I tried some more words in Russian but they did not seem to register at all. Dagir explained loudly and cheerfully in faltering English that he came with a good heart, that he loved England, Folly Farm, and that he wished luck for this time together when we would be friends. They gave me a video of a film shot in their mountains – mournful, Armenian music,

Above left: Broken leg, snow, new ponies, no common language – the first day's rehearsal with Tamerlan. (Toti Gifford)

Above right: Tamerlan, Dagir and Albert (left to right) try on their costumes. (Giffords Circus collection)

Above: Still on crutches. Tamerlan and I in discussion. (Giffords Circus collection)

endless mountains more wild and gigantic than the Scottish Highlands, horses, and more mountains. We put it on, watched a little bit of it and they pointed out their village and the horses, and watched with me. Albert's eyes misted over.

I tried to discuss the ponies with Tamerlan. Yes, good ponies. *Horooshow* 'Good'. Young ponies. Five years old. I have been riding them. Riding. Working. *Roboton* 'work'. One month *roboton* here. We were nervous with each other. We probably agreed to understand each other much more than we actually did understand each other. In fact, we certainly understood very little.

When they left the caravan, I suddenly remembered a phrase in Russian that had seemed very beautiful. It was '*Spakoinai noche*', which translates as 'have a peaceful night'. The sound of it evoked sparkling winter snow, Russian *troikas* whisking over white snow in the dead of night taking the fur-clad riders to a peaceful night's sleep.

That was how I remembered the phrase – '*Spakoinai noche*'. Just to say it now takes me back to that strange broken winter in the caravan and the arrival of the Cossacks. As they opened the door of the wagon and were saying goodnight that phrase suddenly came to me and nervously I blurted it out – '*Spakoinai noche*' – and there were, to my amazement, immediate smiles and laughs and nods. That was when I realised that speaking a language was more than just being understood – it was a reaching out, a connection. I think that was one of the biggest lessons of my adult life.

The next day we worked the horses for the first time. Appropriately, it had snowed in the night. '*Dobra ootra*,' I said to them in stables, loudly – 'good morning!'. And this seemed maybe more comprehensible as they all called back, '*Dobra ootra*', as they slung rawhide saddles and bridles over the stable doors and brushed off the ponies, all except Albert who muttered '*Guten morgen*' through his moustache and continued cleaning the very surprised-looking Eclipse with the house vacuum cleaner. I had never in my life seen someone cleaning a horse with a vacuum cleaner, but I didn't have the language to discuss the pros and cons of this grooming method. I was too disabled by my broken leg to get actively involved and Eclipse didn't seem worried, so I left Albert to it. It occurred to me that perhaps Albert, who from then on only spoke to me in German, thought that maybe he was in Germany.

I clambered up to the outdoor school and sat on a chair covered in blankets with my leg up and a Russian dictionary on my lap. They brought the two ponies to the sandy school. They were wearing rustling nylon shell suits, trainers, and hooded tops. They led the ponies not from the shoulder, as is usual in England, but walked in front of them, tugging them along like pack animals, while blowing cigarette smoke through the snowflakes. The ponies, which were not sure about this, kept stopping, as a horse that has been trained to lead from the shoulder will when it is tugged along, and they pulled at them and spoke to them in Russian words and expressions – '*Alii! Alii!*'. Albert was wearing my coat and he said good morning in German again, then looked at me blankly as snowflakes settled on his moustache. He lit a cigarette and leant on the posts by the school, and I was surprised by this passive stance, although of course my English manners stopped me from saying anything. Besides, he would not have understood anyway.

They put their strange-looking rawhide saddles onto the ponies. They were Russian trick-riding saddles that had a short bar sticking out the front and back of the saddle. Each saddle had a number of girths, like a side saddle or a western saddle. It occurred to me that it would be a good idea to lunge the ponies in the saddle before they jumped on, and tried to suggest that to them from my blanket-covered chair, frantically flicking through the dictionary to find a word for lunge. Maybe they didn't even have that word in Ossetia, I suddenly thought, or maybe it is something different; the literal translation of 'lunge' (lurch forward) may be quite different from its equestrian meaning – to work a horse in a circle on a rope. If I asked them to 'lunge' the pony I might be asking them to lurch forward at the pony, which would be ridiculous.

But in any case, events moved faster than my translation attempts, and Tamerlan in one easy flick of his thin body had jumped onto Red. Dagir jumped onto Rooster. Rooster suddenly decided that things were moving too fast for him, that these strange men smelt odd and sounded odd, that they rustled and smoked and led him in a completely different way to what he was used to, and that in fact he totally objected to this new treatment. He put down his head, went into one massive, unbroken, unbridled honking bronk and left Dagir on the floor in the snow. Rooster then proceeded to jump clean out of the school, galloped all around the farm, head down, girths and stirrups flying, with Tamerlan and Dagir running after him through the snow, shell suits positively singing and cigarette packets flying from every pocket.

Over the next few months we worked intensively together on training the horses

I realised that speaking a language was more than just being understood – it was a reaching out, a connection.

ready for the start of rehearsals in April. From that first disastrous morning onwards the boys trained the ponies in our barn. I sat either in the caravan, plastered leg up, writing notes and planning the show, or in the barn on a chair, leg up, watching them train. I could not walk without crutches and the recovery of my broken leg was very slow and very painful.

'This is a very serious accident,' said Tamerlan with the gravitas of a circus artiste who has worked through numerous injuries. He told me about a broken leg he had sustained a few years ago. I asked him how he had recuperated, and he replied, bafflingly, by running.

That first morning with Rooster had created a problem. Rooster refused to let Tamerlan or Dagir get on him, and whenever they so much as put their hands on the front of the saddle he started to buck. I could see that Tamerlan, who as troupe leader would have to rectify the problem, was not collecting the reins in his left hand to establish contact with the mouth from the ground – the reins were hanging loose and Tamerlan was grasping the bar at the front of the saddle. Rooster ran backwards, or darted forwards, and Tamerlan had no control over him. The problem was not Tamerlan's skill as a horseman – it was converting the training and handling methods with which Rooster was familiar, to a completely different Russian style. Communication was slow and imperfect. Albert smoked, and Dagir jogged around

the outside of the school in a symphony of rustling shell suit. Elena stood well back in the corner, silent and judgemental, and rocked the baby in her arms. Tamerlan struggled on. We were getting nowhere. Sometimes I watched. Sometimes I went back to the caravan and called my aunt and Oliver for advice.

The other pony, Red, took to the work more easily, and within a few days he was declared ready. It just seemed haphazard. Every time I went into the stables Albert was wearing a different article of my clothes – my riding boots, my jacket. He still only spoke German to me. He sat at the end of the barn by the fire, staring his far-away stare and blowing smoke into the cold air. I wanted to say that Albert should be in the ring, helping, or sweeping up, and that they needed to be showing more progress and more routine – but I didn't know how to and, to be honest, I didn't dare.

Within a few days of their arrival they said that they were going to cook a large dinner and serve it by the fire, and that the dinner was part of the funeral arrangements of Albert's cousin. Tamerlan said that in Ossetia a funeral lasts a week and that they continue the wake one day a week, for a month after that. It was a Friday night and Toti and I said that we would give them a lift down to Bourton-on-the-Water to buy food for the dinner the next day, after morning practice. They asked if there was a sauna in Bourton, and we explained that there was one, beside the swimming pool. The next day, at the agreed time, we drove around the barn to the bottom yard where the caravans were. Tamerlan appeared in his smart suit and pointy shoes.

'Two minutes, two minutes,' he said.

We waited for ages – ten minutes. I went back and knocked again. Albert appeared in his smart suit and pointy shoes followed by Dagir.

'Two minutes, two minutes.'

Fifteen minutes later we were off down the drive with a car full of smoking Cossacks. The swimming pool and sauna were right beside the supermarket. It was about noon. A sauna and a shop – this would take, I guessed, about two hours.

'When shall we pick you up?' I asked. 'When shall we come?'

'What?' asked Tamerlan, leaning forward in his seat. Albert stared out the window.

'When pick-up?' I said.

'Now?' said Dagir, helpfully.

'No, what time we pick up. *Skolka Chas* come back. Time pick-up?'

'Oh! No problem, for us, when you come back?'

'How long sauna?' I asked.

'Five, six hours.'

Five or six hours!?

Their approach to the sauna was quite novel for Bourton-on-the-Water. The sauna is at the back of the pool and is mainly empty or occasionally used by groups of chattering girls, who will sit in the pore-popping heat for a few minutes at most. I suddenly realised that the Cossacks planned to get in there for the rest of the day, and that their rucksacks were most likely full of vodka bottles. I could not negotiate this on their behalf, and so wishing them luck and a good afternoon, we left them in the swimming pool car park.

When we eventually did pick them they inevitably had not made it to the supermarket, but were nonetheless dressed, in high spirits and ready to go. We stopped again at the supermarket and, after what seemed like hours, they emerged with bags and bags of flour, lard and more bottles of spirits.

The cooking that followed was ambitious by any standard, the task further complicated by the fact they were cooking from the tiny kitchens of touring caravans, which are designed for frying eggs and making salads. Nonetheless, throughout the following day huge piles of chicken and carrot

Left: Cossack costumes. (Ari Ashley)

risotto (the horses got through a suspiciously large amount of carrots that winter), flatbreads, loaves, pasta, a whole quartered lamb, roast rabbits, pigeons and pheasant (none of which they could have bought in the local supermarket) started to emerge from the little caravans. By four o'clock we all sat down around the fire in the barn, broke the bread and slowly and mournfully toasted Albert's cousin again and again as Albert's eyes became full of watering memories, his far-away stare coming into focus and then dispersing off again to his distant, lost, mountainous land that ruled his heart and the hearts of all these men.

Albert became more of an issue as the weeks went past. He did, to be fair, ride Eclipse every day; she seemed to like him, and he fed her love with thin strips of carrot every time he walked past her. Tamerlan proudly claimed that Albert had taught her to bow, which he hadn't as she already knew this movement. I showed them a photograph of Eclipse bowing taken in the show the year before but they all shook their heads and said, 'No no, Albert very good'. Albert just stared into the distance. He didn't do anything else. He didn't clean up and he didn't help with Rooster. He was clearly, as Toti pointed out, their Uncle Albert, an old and much-loved man who had once been a Cossack and who had been brought along to help, maybe to get through a bereavement, or maybe to make up the numbers.

I did not feel that Tamerlan was taking a grip of the troupe or of the horses. I had imagined that I would just hand the horses over to him and that he would train them. But the problem of Rooster was not getting any better. A week had gone past and Albert just smoked and Rooster still ran backwards or bronked every time they tried to get on him. I spoke to my Aunt Theresa on the telephone daily and her advice was to train the pony four or five times a day in short bursts. I could not

believe that I had ended up with a broken leg, issuing training schedules to Tamerlan.

I spoke to Olga on the telephone and she reassured me, saying that it was going to be hard, but it would be worth it. She said that in the end it would be beautiful. She said that it was like cutting diamonds. She offered to come and translate for me. My notes for that meeting between Olga, Tamerlan and myself clearly revealed the frustrations.

'I need a translator as I feel that otherwise I am just giving orders and I hate this. I have worked for circus companies myself in all capacities and I hate to be a hated boss. But I do expect things to be done in a certain way. Utility room clean, hay nets higher. Albert – is he too old? I have written a script around the idea of young men as it is young men that came for the original meeting in London.'

Tamerlan, Olga and I sat in my caravan and went through these points. We seriously discussed the possibility of sending Albert home and replacing him with a younger and more motivated rider. The prospect obviously troubled Tamerlan deeply.

'This has to work else we are all out of a job,' I said. 'They must keep training even if it is ten times a day. I assumed that they would take control of the horses and this is not how it turned out.'

I remember the meeting – Olga fiercely defending the boys, me trying to explain that I was not attacking them, Tamerlan seeming to understand everything that I said anyway. Long explanations from Olga in Russian. Tamerlan listening and then drooping his eyes to the table and inhaling deeply, sounding frustrated, me terrified that I was losing him in the process. Elena sitting apart, or standing in the corner with their baby, silent and furious.

'Sweep up after practice, clean utility room, clean tack, hay nets high. Albert must stop tying Eclipse's double bridle in a big knot after practice. The leather

is English leather not rawhide and it will damage it. He must stop wearing all my clothes. When my leg is better I will need my coats and boots again.'

The strain was showing for Tamerlan at that point. There he was, thousands of miles from home with a make-shift Cossack troupe – his Uncle Albert and Dagir, the local wide boy, roped in for the contract.

'OK Nell, we start, OK make new, these things.'

The next day, practice started again in earnest with Rooster. They worked him five times a day for short bursts. I sat in a chair by the fire in the rehearsal barn and watched. Progress was slow but it seemed that, gradually, the boys and the ponies were bonding, and that the ponies were getting used to the new way of being handled. However, Albert was showing no greater signs of activity. He still addressed me in German every morning and he still

insisted on tying my precious, under-oiled, double bridle in a huge knot after practice. He sat by the fire staring into the flames, his wide-apart eyes shining, his alabaster face expressionless. I once found him sitting in our caravan watching the video of his mountains, unstirred by me crashing through the door on my crutches.

It was around that time that I lost my temper with the boys. It was, I think, to do with Albert. I felt that my attempts to instruct them politely were being ignored, maybe laughed at. I confronted Tamerlan, shouting at him with all my force and with all my voice, with the other two stood by in shifty attendance. The next day hay nets were strung up as high as washing lines, the barn was swept to a glass sheen, the tack was oiled and, moreover, the yard had an atmosphere of cheering co-operation, which rung out each morning with warm greetings. A better routine established itself on the yard, and Rooster started to relax during the training sessions. There is a time for everything. There is a time to be quiet and a time to shout. And I had just discovered that, once in a while, there is only one way with a stubborn Russian, and that it is to shout your lungs out, then balance is achieved.

Try that trick with a sensitive French clown or a musician – they will walk out the door and you won't see them again. But these were hard men from Allah's war-torn mountains, neighbours with the Chechens, patriarchal, martial. As a polite English girl with a broken ankle, I was going to have to prove myself to them as surely as they were going to have to prove themselves to me.

We got on. The pointy shoes disappeared back into the packing cases and the floor outside the utility room was littered with the standard Russian sportsmen's footwear – rubber flip flops in all sizes, Nike trainers, and little slipper-like black shoes for training in.

'They are real third-world horsemen,' my friend Oliver observed, in his characteristic slow, quiet drawl, eyes half-closed, blonde hair full of sawdust – he and Toti had been tree felling all day. It was an evening in spring and they had just worked the horses. Tamerlan was practising his whip cracking in the barn. He had a 4-foot-long rawhide whip that cracked louder than a shotgun going off. He turned to Oliver and offered him the whip.

'You can do it?'

Oliver was walked into the middle of the barn and flung the whip out to the side to its full reach, pulled it in, snapped it back and bang, the whip cracked. Through the tall wooden doors of the barn the cold was melting to a quietly chattering spring.

In a few weeks Rooster had accepted Tamerlan, and before long both ponies were flying around the ring in the barn with Tamerlan jumping on and off them, standing on two ponies with a foot on each, cantering them in a neat circle. Sunlight poured down from the roof of the barn into the ring. The three boys practised for the first time in full costume. They wore great shaggy sheep-skin waistcoats, a neat red-and-gold coat for Tamerlan, all with leather gaiters and silk trousers and black silk bandanas. They were a vision of flashing eyes and bearded faces, the ponies dressed in cow hides and bridles with metal work, as they did their tricks with shouts and hollers in a Russian tongue, fiercely glaring at each other. Tamerlan stood on the two red ponies, his coat billowing behind him, the other two men in attendance. Albert looking like he had stepped right off the Mongolian Steppe with his blackened eyebrows and moustache and his wide flat eyes, Dagir playing the hard man with pursed lips and strong stance, the weeks of training showing in his arms, the dust from the horses rising about them, Russian rock music echoing from a ghetto blaster. Elena bounced the baby on her knee and smiled from a distance and when Toti and I looked at each other, we saw in each other's eye that gleam which needs no words.

By Easter the act was nearly ready. The days were longer, the weather warmer. On Easter day we all cooked – flatbreads, lamb and potatoes with carrot risotto and chicken, and ate at the table by the fire. We laughed and joked, swapping toasts, Russian words and English words.

Feeling slightly ridiculous I stood by the fire and solemnly delivered the following speech, hoping that this was somehow in tune with Cossack formalities and rituals. Olga was there with some of her Borzoi dogs and, draped in fur coats, she sat to the side of the fire and translated:

'I would like all three men, Dagir, Tamerlan and Albert to come to join us for the whole season, and no other Cossack Dzigit to join them.

Right: Details of The Cockerel Show development work. (Giffords Circus collection)

'I wish them and all of us luck for the season.

'I would like Dagir, Tamerlan and Albert to be presented as Dzigits in the programme.'

The boys wryly acknowledged this speech. I think that they probably thought I was rather silly in my formality. Their codes and rituals were of importance between them, but I had the feeling that they laughed at any attempts to meet ritual with ritual – but their chivalrous courtesy towards me and general basic wish to keep things moving in the right direction meant that they at least feigned a kind of solemn respect for these well-meant words.

After lunch we walked about the garden and looked at the vegetable patch, which we had just started planting, along with some new fruit trees. The grounds were full of stones and piles of rubble; it was still a half-bombed-out demolition site – but the form of a pretty, abundant garden was emerging. Elena walked at twenty paces behind us with the baby, and the men told us about their homes and their gardens so many miles away in the Caucasus. That afternoon spent walking about the rubbly grounds in the early watery light of the year was a moment that stays in my mind, clear, fresh and full of promise – a charmed moment.

Above: Cossacks on tour. My sister Clover ran a backstage cafe called Coco's Cafe. It was used by the Cossacks for vodka drinking and endless games of Connect 4. (Nell Gifford)

The end of the opening night of The Cockerel Show in Hay-on-Wye. A full tent emptying out into the glassy Welsh evening light, an excited public standing in clusters discussing the show, looking at our wagons, buying posters and leaving in fast-stepped laughing groups making for the pubs of Hay, over the river that runs between the circus and the little town, wide and bountiful and beautiful, dotted with rocks and dancing mosquitoes. A few members of the public linger around the circus, politely and curiously eyeing the gaps between the caravans trying to catch one more glimpse of the Cossack that had whirled before their eyes for a moment in the show, one sight of a pony, a bit more eye contact with the circus people, to carry away with you a smile or a wink, and an invitation to join, to run away. But mainly the little village of the backstage just quietly turns in on itself. Later the tent men will leave the ground in smart shirts and gusts of aftershave to join the crowds in the bars and try their hand at whatever the night has to offer, which is mainly pints of dark beer, talk, and a look at the landlord's son's mobile phone with its proud picture of a poached salmon the length of a kitchen table, perhaps a late-night lock-in, perhaps a front room that doubles as an antiques shop merrily thrown open, and glasses of fizzy wine offered amongst pungent candles and piles of Welsh blankets.

Backstage there is a queue for the first shower. Groups of artistes stand in towels and flip flops. The shower door bangs open and shut, steam billowing into the fresh air as make-up and sweat are rinsed off thirty tired people. In the awnings of the Russian caravans barbeques are lit. The pet cat and dog are out, relaxing, in the fading evening sunlight. Children sit quietly in the awnings as the food sizzles. Music and radios play from the doors of the wagons and caravans. Folk flip flop up through the lines of caravans carrying their washbags. Evening plans are discussed. The last few technicians emerge from the tent with bags of rubbish. The box office is locked up.

At the top of the backstage area which slopes steeply up the hill, the horses are put to bed – Tamerlan winds up the bandages, Dagir shoves hay into the stables with a pitchfork and closes the stable door, whistling and chatting to the ponies. Albert stares across the backstage and the tent to the Welsh mountains beyond. There is chatter and excitement in the stables. The stable team now consists of: the three Cossacks; Emily Campbell – a darkly beautiful opera singer and farmer's daughter with an upbringing in military riding; and Nicky de Neuman – an urchin from the backstreets of Covent Garden who stands up on her horse and sings cockney love songs to a melting audience.

'Hello Nelly,' says Nicky, 'did you know that Dagir has just had twins? TWINS! We didn't even know he was married and now he has two babies! Tonight they are going to name the twins.'

There was laughter and commotion amongst the boys, and Dagir with his pursed smiling lips and band-boy swagger greeted me with the swelling pride of a new father.

'Yes I have twins now. Now we must name them!'

Nicky and Emily laughed as they fed their horses and raked up the stables.

'Never mind the mother, eh? She has no say in it I suppose,' they said in dropped voices and quick words so the boys wouldn't understand.

'Yes, I have twins, thank Allah,' Dagir announced to the mountains and the bright spring night.

That night Dagir and Tamerlan were up until very late, the little light in the caravan

window bright, long after the midnight closing down of the site, long after the slurry chats of people getting back from town. In the morning they emerged from the caravan triumphant – the matter concluded.

'So what do you reckon they called the twins?' Nicky asked the next morning as she unlaced the stable tent.

'What?' I responded.

'Tamerlan and Dagir!'

We worked with Tamerlan Berezov for two seasons. Together we entertained over 100,000 people. The ponies learnt to take carrots from the Cossacks' lips and before long Tamerlan announced that Rooster was his brother. Albert did go back to Russia in the end – his melancholy did not lift and he missed his mountains. A younger Georgian Cossack, a ballerina and rider, replaced him. Dagir cooked carrot risotto all season for anyone who called in at his caravan, which soon became known as Dagir's disco. Tamerlan withdrew slightly from the troupe, and gave up drinking. Elena got pregnant and had a son. Tamerlan turned to God, who he was sure had given him a son in his renouncing of alcohol.

We worked together for two seasons and we still stay in touch. God, Allah, vodka, the mountains – the boys left indelible footprints across Giffords Circus. They have gone back to the Caucasus now, and though Russian rock music no longer echoes around the barn I occasionally find little reminders of them – a bit of horse harness carefully mended with strips of rawhide, a stray flip flop. Something of their spirit remains, and I am very grateful for that. I go into each new season with a greater confidence and a more open heart.

Above left: The Cockerel Show banners. (Giffords Circus collection)

Above right: Maureen Poulter, our fan, with Cossack Ruslan. (Giffords Circus collection)

Right: Emily Campbell, opera singer, as starry-eyed stooge and Tamerlan on Rooster and Red. (Giffords Circus collection)

CATCHING FIRE
THE COCKEREL SHOW AND BEYOND

The 2004 Pearl Show – dark and mysterious, black magic and superstition. A company divided and resentful by the end. There was trouble in the company. Something needed sweeping out, some windows needed opening to let in the air and blow away stale air and stuck spirits; something had to change. The last night of the season – trampled sawdust, takeaway pizzas, whispered confessions, Pierrot's make-up lying in streaks on discarded tissues, plaster pearls no longer precious props but discarded rubbish, the minute moments between people that repeat and repeat on tour, played out for the last time and vanished.

Meanwhile, in the southern states of the old Russian Empire, a band of Ossetian Cossacks were making plans to bring their saddles, costumes, families, weapons, their arcane performance style, their strange Alanian folk dances and their ancient training methods across Europe to a previously unheard-of show, in a corner of the United Kingdom, called Giffords Circus.

At the same time, another satellite was revolving around our little planet – a famous Brazilian radical female clown called Angela de Castro.

Angela de Castro was a director. She was also friends with Barry Grantham and had worked with him many times. I was starting to realise that Barry, as choreographer, needed a director alongside him. I can say this with some sort of authority now, as I have learnt a lot in the last ten years

about putting shows together, and these are some very basic principles of show making. But then, I was just feeling my way; working things out as I went. At that stage it had not even occurred to me and Toti that our correct title was 'producer', that as 'director of horse sequences' and 'costume designer and supervisor', as I could have also called myself, and Toti as 'head of logistics' or 'technical manager', we were effectively hiring ourselves. For, whether we knew it or not, our crucial first and last role, is that of producer.

So we hired Angela de Castro as director. She made one major and profound change to the company. It was a change that we will never reverse. It took a lot of work, planning and upkeep – it still does – and it took about two years to implement, but it is an absolutely essential part of Giffords Circus. It is what helps to make the effect of Giffords Circus – the sense of inclusion, of unlimited possibility, of joy, of surprise. She made Giffords Circus into an ensemble company.

This is what I remember about my early work with de Castro, a very short rounded figure with huge surprised eyes and a shaved head. She said that when we stood side by side we made the number ten. That used to make her laugh a lot. We were always standing side by side, watching people performing. She said we must look very funny.

We were sitting in the little first-floor office in the Dutch barn, looking out into the curved steel trusses and roosting pigeons. Down below was the main barn. The Cossacks were due to arrive in a few

Left: Nancy Trotter in The Cockerel Show. (Giffords Circus collection)

weeks. Somewhere a radio was playing. The fire in the big barn was glowing. I said something about a clown walking along a rope on the ground as if it were a tight wire.

'A totally unoriginal idea,' she said.

We sat some more, thinking. I said that I had taught my horse Eclipse to lie down.

'That is very good. So you should ask Eclipse what will happen next.'

This is the way our conversations progressed. I remember she said once that I was an artiste with a very interesting intellect. I feel so grateful for de Castro for spending this time with me, because she was one of the first people, after Barry, one of the first proper theatre practitioners, to take me seriously. And the confidence that this gave me, the sense that I could move forward, and should, and had something to say that was of interest, this confidence – it makes or breaks.

De Castro had been involved, amongst many other works, with creation at Cirque du Soleil, and had originated a clown character for a very famous and influential Russian clown called Slava. She had performed in his Snow Show for two years. It was de Castro who said that I was an artiste in progress and should be careful. I think by this she meant that I was still forming ideas and identity, and every move and decision would affect the outcome. De Castro said that our company was nearly an ensemble. She said that if we wanted to make a true ensemble then everyone would need to participate in everything. The artistes, all of them, would need to do the singing and dancing and movement exercises along with the core company members – Nancy, Izzy, Tweedy and so on. She also said that our weekly company meeting had stagnated. The company would troop into the tent, sit around the ring, and then everyone would start to complain about the rubbish, the state of the loos. In fact it had got to the point where we just met each week in the

tent on tour to discuss how clean the loos were. It was miserable and depressing.

'Get everyone on their feet,' she said. 'No sitting down. Do not say a single negative thing. Get them to play ball, make it fun. Ball is a good game because you have to work together as a team. You have to be the group. The whole group has to work to keep the ball in the air.'

These were revelations indeed, golden advice.

Early in our work together we hired de Castro to run her clown workshop for us. The participants were our musicians, two of the girls in the office, the dark-eyed opera singer Emily, Tweedy, a girl who was going to assist in the wardrobe, and a few others. What I remember is de Castro insisting that I participate. I had said to her that I was thinking of withdrawing from performing in the show and she was fiercely opposed to this. 'You are a performer. That would be a very bad idea. You would start to feel remote from the show. You must take part in all the workshops. You cannot sit in the corner as you have been. It would not be good for the group.'

So from that moment, I was in. I have subsequently never taken myself out.

I remember feeling very, very nervous in the lead up to the 'Why not?' workshop. I knew that de Castro had trained with Gaulier and that she was going to put us on the spot, that we would not be able to hide from her in the group, and that we would, horror of all horrors, be asked to improvise. What I learnt was that, as with Barry, we were in the hands of a master and that initial embarrassment and self-consciousness fell away as we tried to get to grips with the difficult business of creating comedy, of performing and of working in the present moment. The serious business of being funny.

We did five days of work in the hall. We played, we improvised, de Castro setting up scenarios that we had to work through and

situations that we had to imagine. We had to, one by one, face the group wearing a red nose and maintain eye contact with each person for an unlimited period of time, until something intangible was exchanged through the eye contact. The red nose is a device that blocks the centre of the face and it's true, it reveals the vulnerability in the face. We had to, on another day, stand one by one in front of the group, and within the count of ten seconds do something, anything, that would make people laugh. What I learnt is that there is no possible way that people are going to laugh if you do something shy or half-hearted. The only way is throw yourself off the cliff of embarrassment, and go for it with generosity, imagination and gusto. She taught us how to stand and receive applause, and more mundane things, such as our responsibility to the audience, even after the show, even days after the show, even years. She said that after the Snow Show she felt so tired

when people would come to the stage door, but that it was her responsibility as a performer to receive their praise with grace. And on the way home on the bus, she was still tired, and people were still wanting to say they loved the show. And even now, she said, years later, they still say it, and it is still her responsibility.

We did a lot of work towards creating a clown character, investigating the curious dignity of a clown getting dressed – trying to look your best. The clown might be wearing a lopsided collection of upside-down undone clothes – but to the clown, they are very smart, their best appearance.

De Castro exploded my anxieties about the cultural barriers between the performers, and between the performers and the creative team (essentially de Castro and I). It was one thing to ask a co-operative, keen clown like Tweedy to do eccentric dance moves, or to ask Izzy, a trained dancer, to do a mime improvisation. But the circus

Above: Catching fire in The Cockerel Show. (Giffords Circus collection)

artistes were different. They often come from a sports background. They are usually very highly trained athletes working in one discipline. They like to be very very good, they do not want to try something that they have not been trained for, and are completely reluctant to let go, to sing or dance. They are locked into their own gymnastic movement. Eastern European circus schools do not have a general programme of movement and acting – it is relentless skill-driving. The cultural barrier was thick, heavy and tall. But de Castro was without hesitation, any fear, or any sense that she would fail, and drove a coach and horses through these barriers.

Above left: Trio Slipchenko in The Cockerel Show. (Giffords Circus collection)

Above right: Me on Eclipse in The Cockerel Show. (Giffords Circus collection)

It took time, partly because our administration had to catch up with this new way. We had to be sure that the artistes were clearly briefed *before* they signed the contract that they would be expected to take part in the ensemble, and that they would be expected to act and sing and dance.

Over the years, Toti and I have gone to great lengths to make sure that this message is understood – we have even travelled to Moscow to sit with a troupe and tell them. But in those early days, around 2005 and 2006, the message did not always get across. This frustrated de Castro.

'You must tell them,' she said. She was absolutely insistent on this. 'You must tell them because otherwise they won't expect it and then they will be separate, and then you have a problem with the company dividing again.'

In 2005 the first performers that de Castro worked with on our behalf were the Cossacks. I remember very clearly first introducing de Castro to Tamerlan. Tamerlan was sitting on his horse in the main barn. It was day time, raining hard outside, the barn gutters gurgling. De Castro and I came through the door from the workshop into the barn. We climbed in the ring and went over to Tamerlan. He was dressed in warm clothes, gloves and a balaclava and he had quite a long beard at that time. He was sitting quite still on his rawhide saddle, looking to all the world like a mounted terrorist.

'Tamerlan, this is de Castro, de Castro, this is Tamerlan. De Castro will be directing.'

'Hello de Castro. This is my horse Rooster. He has no balls. I have two balls.'

De Castro seemed very interested in this introduction, amused and interested, completely unfazed.

Later in the week, while working with the Cossacks, de Castro's wife and two children came to visit. The Cossacks were hard-living patriarchal men from the mountains of the Caucasus. Their culture is many things – resourceful, self-sufficient, proud – but it also is homophobic and racist. I watched the boys looking at de Castro and I wondered how on earth they would ever take leadership from her. But of course, they did. They adored her. De Castro and Tamerlan struck up a real friendship. They made each other laugh a lot. If anything, they were greater friends for their differences.

That is the magic of circus, and that is one of the reasons I love it so much.

Day one of rehearsals.

'Everyone to the tent,' called de Castro. 'Everyone. We are *all* going to learn the choreography and we are all going to learn the songs. It does not matter if they will not be singing in the show. Who knows, maybe they will. Come on, Nell, this is how we will make an ensemble. And you as well, you will learn all the choreographies and songs.'

Another revelation. Get everyone into that tent and work with them all together with everyone on the same level.

The first show to come out of this collaboration was called The Cockerel Show. I said that I wanted to write a show about a cockerel. I was inspired by the Cossacks, their strutting machismo, the bright colours of the two chestnut ponies and the bright colours of the Cossacks' regalia. De Castro spent a lot of time in her little studio in Bethnal Green developing the script.

'What I can't see, Nell, is where the cockerel is! There is no cockerel in this Cockerel Show! Listen, I have an idea. What about Tweedy trying to find the cockerel? That is the show – the search for the cockerel. And then we can have a little song at the end called "The Cockerel Song"!'

De Castro started rolling around in her chair and clapping her hands and singing a funny song, which she said was a type of Brazilian tune.

'Da da da da da DAH, da da da da da da DAH, we are really very happy now the cockerel's in the show.'

So that was what we did. We put chickens in the ring in the pre-show, and Tweedy improvised with them, teaching them, carefully and kindly, to balance on top of a broom. The chickens were happy – so happy that they used to jump out of their carrying box and literally run into the ring where they used to settle down and lay eggs in the sawdust. The Russian Trio, Slipchenko, willingly and gamely dressed as ring boys, and played this to the end where they suddenly burst out of this prosaic role to execute a series of spectacular flips and somersaults off the bar.

The chickens were so happy that they used to jump out of their carrying box and literally run into the ring to settle down and lay eggs in the sawdust.

Right: Dancing girls as cockerels in The Cockerel Show. (Olga Sienko)

The Cossacks taught our chestnut ponies to gallop around the ring, where they jumped on and off in high Cossack style. Tamerlan stood up on his horse while it walked around Nicky de Neuman, equestrian chanteuse, as she stood on her horse, singing. A finer, straighter stand on a horse you could not ask for. Tamerlan filled the ring with his Cossack spirit. Nicky and Emily Campbell played dark-haired passionate love rivals, Emily as audience stooge who sat as an anonymous audience member, only to stand up and start singing the 'Toreador Song' from *Carmen* at full belt. We did a version of 'Roxanne', with a gradual build from one Cossack and one naughty dancer, dancing together with maximum chemistry, to the entire company including the Cossack rider who had burst in to interrupt this passionate duo, all singing together around the ring.

I had had a brilliant time that year working with Becky at Bristol Costume Services – we had visited a backstreet holstery fabric shop and, rather than buying fabric specifically for a costume, we bought a mountain of cheap, garish, madly patterned upholstered fabric, fabric that we decided worked for the show, but in a vague and impressionistic way – and we then worked the costumes up out of this.

The show ended as it had begun, with a burst of choreography and all the company appearing in these colourful costumes, bedecked with ribbons, pompoms and coloured ropes, and carrying colourful banners. Tweedy stripped off his blue ring-boy costume to reveal an identical ring-boy costume, only this version in gold spandex. It was a sexy, short, colourful show, and then we did a wild eccentric dance, pure Barry Grantham, with the dancers all dressed as burlesque chickens.

Participation in this ensemble was not accepted by the whole company, and in 2005 there were still problems, but I do think that this was the year that we caught fire. The Cossacks were ridiculously good fun to work with. Dagir was a bon viveur first and last. In a Cossack caravan, a bottle of vodka, a piece of cheese and a tomato became a party. There were still problems, yes, but the psychological black hole that we had all ended up in at the close of The Pearl Show 2004 had gone. We started to find a pace and a style of our own, and I felt that de Castro had given me tools for managing the company, tools that I would have to learn how to use, but would serve me well. We were less nostalgic this year, more dashing, in a way more grown up. I remember Izzy standing in the barn looking at the Cossacks and then looking at me and saying that she loved it, the new style.

'Yeah, Nell,' she said, 'it's more sexy isn't it, more rock and roll.'

It was a new direction, but it was fun, and it felt right. At the end of The Cockerel year we rehired the Cossacks, the band, the Trio Slipchenko, Tweedy of course, Emily and Nicky. Izzy and Rebecca moved on to other shows and to develop their own work. We found an incredible Russian family who did an old-fashioned act called a Rizley act – basically foot juggling each other. De Castro and Barry Grantham agreed to come on board again. I decided to call the 2006 show Joplin!, and it was to be about Janis Joplin – her life and work.

I think that Joplin! was the first year that we were finally united and uncorked.

10

JOPLIN!
GIFFORDS CIRCUS UNCORKED

My idea for Joplin! was that the whole circus was a sort of early 1960s nightclub, and that all the performers were to be, in one way or another, musicians.

I developed this show on my own, more or less, and while researching Janis Joplin, I fell in love with the music of Orleans, in particular the funeral procession jazz bands – 'the second liners'. These are walking players, who walk behind in the 'second line' of New Orleans funeral processions and play in a very specific and unique syncopated brass style. I found a documentary made by Alan Yentob. I became fixated by these deep Southern blues roots of the modern American rock sound that Janis Joplin was an early exponent of, and I became determined to find some real New Orleans second-line trombone players to bring to the UK for the show. I suppose that the work with the Cossacks had given me a confidence in being able to collaborate with international 'world' performers, not just circus acts, and I wanted to learn more.

We had just moved into our new house at Folly Farm. We had a big bedroom and a spare room, which was for children; we didn't have children, though very much wanted them, and so I used the spare room as a make-shift office. I watched that documentary over and over again. Hurricane Katrina had just hit and there was a lot in the news about the devastation of New Orleans. In the documentary it said that a man had been rescued from his home, an anonymous New Orleans resident clinging to his rafters in a waterlogged house, and that man turned out to be Fats Domino. I had a sense of New Orleans being a source, a starting point, a richness of talent.

At the time, we could not afford to travel there and so I worked online trying to source two musicians to join our team of Peter, Bill and Colin. Somehow I made contact with an agent in Chicago. We talked and emailed constantly. Slowly I won his trust and he found me two musicians in New Orleans who were real second-line jazz players. I talked to these two players, emailed and sent them material in the post. They were both homeless after the hurricane and welcomed a short-term job in the UK playing for a circus. It seemed to me to be a great way to offer aid, a job rather than charity; at that moment in time some kind of synchronicity meant that they needed me and I needed them. Slowly, carefully, and with a leap of faith on both sides, we arrived at an agreement. They would come to England and they would join Giffords Circus in 2006.

Disaster struck. The Home Office refused their visa application. Months and months of negotiation down the drain. They had consulted with the Musicians' Union who had said that jazz musicians of this type were already resident in the UK

and so the job should be given to them. We appealed but were turned down. I disagree with the Musicians' Union in this case. The two guys I had found were practising second-line musicians. They could walk and play at the same time and their style is specific to New Orleans – it is world music. I have never since then been able to find a UK musician who is prepared to walk and play at the same, let alone walk and play to a high standard.

Our appeal was futile and my two guys were not coming over. We managed to find two substitute musicians through an old friend, great musician and manager Gaz Mayall. But it was not a great start.

Shaken by this episode, which happened very late in the spring toward the start of rehearsals, we began to pull the company together. There was the welcome, poignant return of the Trio Slipchenko family, who came this time with a new partner as Sasha had died over the winter. The new Russian gymnast Rizley act family arrived; they set up in their new caravans and watched proceedings at Folly Farm in that inscrutable Russian way. The Cossacks rolled into town again. Tamerlan brought with him two new boys: languid whip-thin Ossetian ballerinas, brothers called Ruslan and Omar. He had had them all fitted out in Ossetia with brand-new paisley Jimi Hendrix-style shirts and leather belts. They looked unbelievably cool. I was so grateful to Tamerlan. He turned up with such commitment, such gusto, and with that brilliant good humour. He walked into the kitchen at Folly Farm – a scene no doubt of stress and pre-rehearsal chaos, missing musicians, shaky running order, problems with the tent, a hotline to the Home Office – and he exclaimed with his rolling Russian Rs:

Above left: A vintage Janis Joplin tour poster. (Giffords Circus collection)

Above right: Our publicity material. (Design by Windpress)

Above: Drawings towards the show. (Nell Gifford)

'Happy Christmas!'

Nobody had noticed that the top yard, where we put the tent up and the barn stands, where the hay and straw was kept, had suddenly become completely overrun with rats. They were everywhere, scuttling about with that horrible confidence rats have when they know their numbers are swelling. Tamerlan found Toti's air rifle and sat in the barn for the next few days, quietly picking off the rats until there were none left.

Tamerlan, Giffords Circus loves you.

I did a massive amount of research for this show. I found a lot of DVDs of 1960s pop festivals and documentaries about Janis Joplin. I read all her biographies and letters. What I found compelling was her lack of vanity, the fact that she got up on stage and sang, and danced, without worrying if she looked ridiculous or unattractive. She was uncompromising. It was not a matter of styling and angling herself to look as sexy as possible – no, she had something to say and she said it as forcefully as she could. It was interesting to see the footage of the early pop festivals – the disorganisation, the risk-taking – again, completely unselfconscious. I used to play the DVDs of the circus acts we had hired and play iconic 1960s songs over the top of this visual to see how it could work. I watched the Rizley act family over and over again on the DVD they had sent me. The five little figures would walk into the ring in kind of black-and-white space suits, and they would perform their incredible gymnastic act punctuated with very Russian-looking choreographies, the circling of arms.

I played 'Going Up the Country' by Canned Heat, 'Marrakesh Express' by Crosby, Stills and Nash, and Janis Joplin's 'Train' over the top of this. It looked weird and experimental. It was perfect. For my own act on Eclipse I chose 'Thank you for the Days' by The Kinks.

It made me think about my mum a lot and I used this feeling to find the atmosphere for the act – celebrational, wistful but optimistic. Days I remember all my life. This is what is so strange about putting shows together.

I didn't really *know* that my mum liked this song. And I didn't set out when Toti and I hit upon the idea of Janis Joplin to delve into my parents' late 1960s and 1970s music. But somehow this is what came up.

I remember that Joplin! rehearsals were fairly stressful. The show was formless, a psychedelic flow of images and ideas. De Castro suggested that we take a photograph of every company member and put it up on a board in the main barn so that everyone would know who each other was.

Above left: Joplin! rehearsals. (Andrew Rees)

Above right: The Slipchenkos. (Andrew Rees)

Right: Working
with milliner
Noël Stewart.
(Andrew Rees)

Matt Driver
Kitchen Gangster

Tamerlan Berezov
"Captain of Troupe Tamerlan"
cossack rider

James
carpenter

"Wayne"
Painter at Folly Far

Simon Lovelace
Light + Sound

Ian Rumbelow
Tent / stage manager

Baki Translator.

Andrew Rees
Photographer

"Dan"
Carpentry

Omar Tarba
Cossack rider

"Rockey"
Carpentry + "handyman"
x

Maciej Kaliszewicz
Stable Assistant / Logistical
support

Philip Risley Act.

Valeria Risley Act.

Agnieszka Kaliszewicz
Assistant / Logistical support

"Alfie"
Accounts

Sasha
Russian Bar

Tweedy
The clown.

Gusha
Risley Act.

Bill Harbottle
Musician

BiBi Juggler.

Natalia
Hula-Hoop

Valentina
Risley Act.

Pete sen
Musical Director

Stuart Driver
Sous scrubber!

Sarah Mcmorrine
Katy's Assistant / Front of
House.

Andre Russian Bar.

Marek Niedzwiecki
General Assistant / Driver
Tent crew.

Andre Bassing
Musician - (Jazz Pianist)

Juggler Bichu

Geoff Marching Band.

Valerie
Risley Act.

My old friend Jacqui Harrison and I built some backboards that had the words ART IS LIFE against a shiny foil background. We made some curious mesh fish on bamboo poles, and decorated umbrellas in a New Orleans funeral procession style. Felt, beads, my old blue starry flares, the Cossacks' Jimi Hendrix shirts. It poured with rain at Folly and rehearsals were wet and muddy. It was a dark, damp dress rehearsal and Nicky had quite a bad fall from her horse in the tent. A difficult opening in Hay-on-Wye – more mud, more wet. The show took about three weeks to run in and for that time it felt shaky.

But during the course of the season the company gelled together. Tweedy, Bibi and Bichu did some brilliant joint comedy and juggling. The Cossacks flew. The Rizley family brought the house down with their breathlessly brilliant and terrifying gym-

nastics, getting standing ovations again and again. By the end of the season we were a company that was moving as one. We were complete. We knew what it was to deliver a show as an ensemble, with no reluctance from anyone, with the whole company playing as one. The Russians bought into the ensemble, they went with it, dancing and acting and smiling. The musicians found perfect timing behind each act. Giffords Circus uncorked.

The following year, 2007, we did not tour. I can say that we were, by the end of 2006, burnt out. I was shattered. We had toured non-stop for seven years, built a farm, a house and a company with a growing international reputation and a performance culture of its own to maintain. I felt that I had run out of momentum and new ideas. And there was something else pressing. We wanted to start a family.

Above: Bibi and Bichu. (Andrew Rees)

Right: Katy Kelly as Janis. (Andrew Rees)

Left to right: Me, Emily Campbell and Omar. (Andrew Rees)

Left: Sarah Duddy,
one of the dancers.
(Andrew Rees)

Right: Our poster –
psychedelic Eclipse.
(Andrew Rees)

Tweedy.
(Andrew Rees)

The Aloshin family
and their Rizley
act. (Andrew Rees)

Giffords Circus 2006. (Giffords Circus collection)

NIGHTS AT THE CIRCUS

Circus nights in Circus Roncalli, way back in 1998. The days were hot, the work continuous, but the evenings were sweet – warm dark nights, sitting outside Csuba's little caravan, eating hot greasy goulash soup, drinking red wine and talking about music.

The circus is not particularly a place for sleeping. There is always someone awake, always the sound of a telly, a stereo, people talking, a generator, a dog barking. I know that I sleep less deeply at the circus, in a little wagon that rocks and creaks in the wind and that the rain drums on, than I do in the solid walls and silence of a house. It is surprising how much quieter houses are, how well bricks and mortar screen sound as well as weather. But this makes the circus a companionable place – there is generally always someone awake to talk to. It is a place where it is very easy to burn the candle at both ends.

Our generator goes off at midnight, although there is twenty-four-hour power for the people with children. Until the generator goes off, if it is nice weather, people sit outside. Barbeques are an essential part of circus life, as are homemade cocktails, sitting around in deck chairs looking at the stars and watching movies together, sometimes projected onto the walls of the tent. The diligent Ukrainians practise after the show, they go back into the ring with exercise mats and stereos and work out and train new acts. People go to the pub, or look for nice restaurants. Our travelling circus restaurant is usually full of people eating bowls of stew and rice and vegetables, excited after the show. Sometimes the villages we visit are so excited by the circus presence that they throw parties, and the dark summer air is full of music.

Left: Giffords Circus wagon. (James Waddell)

Right: Minchinampton Common. (Andrew Rees)

I remember sitting on the edge of the Hay Castle ground outside one of the performer's caravans. The ground there is sort of elevated up above pavement level and so through the tangly perimeter hedge you could see people walking to the Hay Festival events or into town, amid traffic. I absolutely love that – the circus in the town – the quiet domesticity of the circus and its animals in close juxtaposition with town life. I associate that deeply with Circus Roncalli.

I think that some grounds have their own energy. The ground at Lechlade is an old monastery site that was used as a hospital for returning crusaders in the days when Lechlade was an important inland port. It has a feeling of ground that has been inhabited for centuries, well trodden, well occupied. We have spent many happy weeks with the circus at The Trout Inn in Lechlade. Many wild excursions upstream with the whole company in a hired boat, much wilder swimming, walks in the meadows, night-time drinks outside the pub listening to jazz and the sound of the weir. Minchinhampton nights on that high dry chalk pasture, watching shooting stars and listening to Minchinhampton church bells, Marlborough, the end of the season, chilly nights and excursions to the Italian restaurant, Pino's, in town, and then the long pasta-laden red wine climb up the hill to bed.

Circus days are so full, so busy. The whole day is timed to the show. So what you do at nine o'clock in the morning relates to the unshakable deadline of the five o'clock show. This makes circus nights a time to freewheel, to talk, to confide, to see the other side of things.

Below: Dancers. (Giffords Circus collection)

Right: The back door of Circus Sauce. (Giffords Circus collection)

But they go by like the sea going away from the stones, and leaving only the stones tinkling in your eyes and ears

(Giffords Circus collection)

"There is pansy that's for thoughts."

The word pansy comes from the French word penseé meaning thought. The pansy has long been a symbol of free thought. In William Shakespeare's play "A Midsummer Night's Dream" the juice of a pansy blossom is a love potion "the juice of it, on sleeping eyelids laid, will make a man or a woman madly dote upon the next live creature that it sees." If you find a pansy left for you by a secret admirer, it would mean "I am thinking of our forbidden love." Grow your own pansys from these seeds; and handle the petals with care.

11

BRASS BANDS AND PANSIES
THE END OF INNOCENCE

Sometime during that year off in 2007 I went to Paris to see a friend. I also visited Le Crazy Horse de Paris dance show. I remembered that Izzy had mentioned a choreographer called Molly Molloy, and I knew that Molly Molloy worked at Le Crazy Horse as the dance director and I was intrigued. During that visit I spent quite a lot of time wandering about the Left Bank. The Left Bank generally refers to the Paris of an earlier era; one that symbolised intellect and scholarship, where writers, poets, artists and philosophers flocked to sit in the numerous cafes, creating a bohemian culture and a great artistic community. Although the Left Bank now boasts some of the most expensive properties in Paris, and is a place of serious high-end fashion, there are still the cafes and a sense of counterculture and creativity clinging to the winding streets and bustling boulevards.

One day I was walking along the Rue Bonaparte towards the church of St-Germain-des-Prés when I heard the sound of a loud, mad, very jolly, tin can brass band. I was drawn to the sound of this band. As I got closer I saw a group of scruffy-looking students with battered old brass instruments playing for all they were worth to a group of tourists. It was an irresistible sound. It made you feel happy, it made you want to dance. It was so loud, so unabashed, so unpolished. I loved it. I stood and

Left: Designs and ideas for 2008. (Nell Gifford)

watched them for some time. I then walked back to my hotel with a vague idea of finding one of my cards or an old programme to give to them. By then Toti and I had a lot of experience with travelling around circus schools finding acts, but we had never actually a picked an act up off the street. I don't know why now, but I was hesitating.

When I arrived back at the pretty little square, the tables outside Les Deux Magots, a famous cafe that was renowned as being the rendezvous point for the intellectual and literary elite of the city, were still full of chic Parisians, talking, drinking coffee and reading papers, but the musicians had moved on. I think I felt relieved that I would not have to steel myself to walk up to them and talk to them as a complete stranger, but at the same time I was annoyed with myself for letting them go.

Later that evening I was walking along the Rue des Beaux-Arts back to the hotel where I was staying, L'Hôtel – an exquisitely beautiful backstreet hotel – and I heard the music again, this time ahead of me and moving away from me. My card and programme were in my pocket and so, feeling brave, I ran after the sound. They were walking along in a row on the narrow pavements playing away on their instruments. It was not a sophisticated sound but it filled the dark narrow streets again. I caught up with the player at the end of their little procession. He was a cherub-faced young

205

boy with a kind of homemade drum kit strapped around his neck.

'Hello, hello,' I said, 'please take this.'

He stopped and smiled and took the card and little coloured programme.

'Hello, sorry, I don't speak French, but I love what you are playing.'

By now the other players had stopped, walked back down the pavement and were gathering around. A beautiful dark-haired girl, a red-headed boy, a girl with glasses and plaits. They looked very much like French arts students. They were smiling and friendly.

'Look, I like your music. I have a circus. Please call me, if you want. All the details are there.'

'OK! Great! Yes we will. We will. Thank you very much.'

'Thank you! Call me!'

We went our separate ways. I went back to my hotel and went to bed. I did not really expect to hear from them again.

La Fanfare Suivante is a student brass band. It was set up by a group of students from the École Nationale Supérieure des Beaux-Arts in St-Germain, reviving a student tradition of brass bands. They busked around the streets of the Left Bank, partly to raise cash, but also because the streets were somewhere they could practise.

After that initial meeting the group did get in contact. I explained to them by email from England about our little show, and I said how much I liked their music. We were planning a new show for 2008. Both Toti and I felt that we needed a new element, that we should to some extent reinvent the show. Our drummer Peter Sen had got married and settled down in Cheltenham, and Colin and Bill had moved on. A new musical set-up was needed. Toti and I travelled over to Paris to meet the

band again. This time we met them first in the great studios of the art school, and second in the little cafe beside the L'Hôtel on the Rue des Beaux-Arts. With each meeting their numbers swelled. They were bright, articulate, well-educated people. They seemed eager to join us. We said that we would have room for eight musicians but they were determined to play en masse and proposed that thirteen of them would come but that they would split the wage for eight people and work out the accommodation between them. They were so keen, so enthusiastic, so well versed in talking about arts projects – I can say we all fell in love with La Fanfare Suivante. Claire, with dark flashing eyes and nonchalant attitude; Jean, red headed and opinionated; baby-face Carlos; Fanny; Mimi; Valentine. They were grown-up children, young people at the start of life, full of boundless enthusiasm, naive, smart, twenty-first century.

While we were in Paris, Toti and I also visited Le Crazy Horse again to try and track down Molly Molloy. We finally made contact with her and she invited us to see her after a show. Le Crazy Horse de Paris is a Parisian cabaret, a boutique burlesque club, frequented by tourists, rock stars and the cream of Parisian chic. Primarily famous for its perfectly synchronised, indistinguishable dancers, it also has been a popular venue for many other artistes including magicians, jugglers and mimes. Set up in 1951 by Alain Bernardin, it is a tiny, very sexy, very adult venue, where you sit on little swivel chairs in booths and confiding waiters serve you champagne as you watch twelve girls, naked save for a spray of coloured lights, do a series of burlesque comic dance numbers. Pure Paris.

Le Crazy Horse is painted throughout with red gloss paint. Underground. Black night. Silk tights and secrets. It is very expensive and it is constantly packed. After the show a cool blonde girl showed

old man on bony
thoroughbred?

Harris Hawk

Harris hawk

lovely Welsh Cobs D

fur

zebra print

bells

each do a solo
passage
piaffe
rear
kneel
spannish walk

All come on in 1st half for
number.
3 horses
dogs
Harris Hawks.

Come on again at end
for wedding.

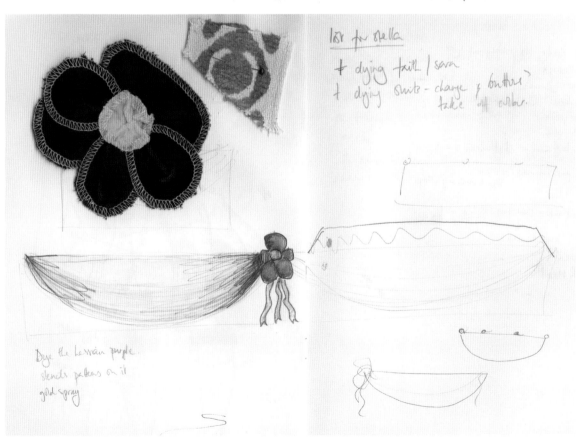

for stella
+ dying tails / sam
+ dying suits - change of buttons?
take off collar.

Dye the hessian purple.
stencils patterns on it
gold spray

us through a little maze of corridors, also painted gloss red, to a sitting area with red velour seats. We waited there for a while. I was wearing very high heels and a dress. Anything less would have felt scruffy. Toti was in his best suit. We sat quietly and looked at the framed black-and-white photographs on the walls.

Molly Molloy appeared around the corner with the cool blonde girl and another assistant. Molly Molloy had chic grey hair, a pretty, rounded face and fierce eyes, and was dressed head to toe in black. I would later learn that she only ever wore black or white. They were talking in French and English. Molly spoke with an American accent. She was very friendly and welcoming. She said that she would love to talk to us but we would have to excuse her because Agent Provocateur were doing a photoshoot and they were also rehearsing a guest singer, a French celebrity. We said to please not worry, we were fine, we were happy sitting there in the cosy red room. It was so interesting, just to be backstage and see how another show operated. Molly said that she would be right back, and she was off. She reappeared ten minutes later and we talked a bit. She said that she had heard about our show and she asked who had put us onto her. She seemed genuinely surprised and flattered that we had come to see her, which I found quite astonishing given her stature as a dance director and choreographer. I said it was Isabelle Woywode, Izzy.

'Ah yes, Izzy!' she said. 'She is so great. Such imagination. Great dancer but more than that, one of those special ones, right?'

And then she was off again at the word of the cool blonde assistant, who we learnt later from Molly was a Polish ex-dancer, trilingual and the *best* assistant she had ever had. I would learn that Molly Molloy had an assistant in every country.

We later talked for some time about Le Crazy Horse. I found out from Molly that the burlesque club, as with most dance shows, has a very strict protocol for performers, including weight control and segregation between performers and front-of-house members of staff. The girls have stage names, different to their own, by which they are known within the building. They are not allowed to talk to the audience, which is important in creating the mystical and magical atmosphere. The conditions are strict, but the girls employed at Le Crazy Horse have an opportunity not just to live and work on such a prestigious show, but also to make a lot of money. Molly told us that Alain Bernardin used to insist on interviewing the girls with their parents present, and when successfully employed would help them to set up a savings account and direct debit, encouraging them to save and build towards owning their own apartments. Today, all over Paris are old ladies, ex-Crazy Horse girls, who live in their chic Parisian apartments.

We also talked about Molly coming to work with us. She agreed in principle.

So we came home from Paris with a brass band and a choreographer/director called Molly Molloy.

The end of innocence. From 2000 to 2006 we were essentially a group of artistes, performers and producers who had a dream and lived the dream. We were in our twenties. We learnt as we went. There were no grown-ups, so to speak. Barry and de Castro had a profound influence on the company but they did not tour with us. During these years we were volatile, excitable and inexperienced. In 2008, we suddenly found that we were the grown-ups. The French band were palpably younger. We had to lead them and guide them and were occasionally disapproving if they were too wild, or too noisy, late at night. Before 2008 there were no noisy, late-night parties – we *were* the noisy late-night party. They were to some extent a new

Left top: Tweedy. (Andrew Rees)

Left bottom: The bear. (Andrew Rees)

generation of performers and company members. And Molly Molloy, where Barry had opened the door to a whole world of movement language, and where de Castro had shown us the way to create ensemble, Molly got a hold of our production process and shook it hard into shape. She came as choreographer, ended up directing, and coached me as producer. That is why 2008 was for me the end of innocence. We could no longer freewheel. We were no longer the *enfants terribles* of the English circus scene. We were grown-up circus producers and had to organise ourselves as such, and if we did not understand that then we did by the time Molly Molloy had finished with us.

The 2008 show was inspired by the story of a fairground girl called Rebecca Biddel. This is an account of her wedding day, from Frances Brown's *Strollers & Showfolk*:

On the thirteenth of December 1894 she walked up the aisle of St. Paul's in Old Brentford with John Francis Stroud, who made his living from coconut shies on the fairground. The bride, giving her occupation as 'theatrical profession', made such an impression in her red velvet dress and large red hat that locals still recalled the event over twenty years later.

I was fascinated to find out that there had been a fairground family with the surname Stroud, as this is my maiden name. I wanted to write a show about the early days of the fair, the fair as a religious holiday, a meeting of all levels in society, a place of entertainment and trade. I tried to imagine this world – the cacophony of stall holders and brass bands and fair organs and animals and show fronts. I wanted to call the circus that year 'Stow Fair' but I worried that this might cause a real confusion as Stow Fair is an actual biannual horse fair that takes place in our local town of Stow-

on-the-Wold. Therefore, we decided to call the show Caravan.

These were some of the elements: a realistic bear costume (this proved to be extremely expensive to make and difficult to engineer) and a scene from Shakespeare. I thought that it was likely Shakespearean players would have played at fairs in Warwickshire or Gloucestershire in mobile fit-ups in the sixteenth century. It seemed plausible and exciting to include a scene from Shakespeare. We chose Ophelia's madness scene from *Hamlet*.

'There is pansies, that's for thoughts'.

The language of flowers. The pansy became a predominant image in the creation of that show. We made velvet pansies and embroidered them with coloured wool. I inherited my mum's old sofa that was upholstered in William Morris fabric. The fabric was threadbare and no longer any good for covering the sofa. I stripped it off, recovered what I could and then lined the back of the pansies in this fabric. Front-of-house staff wore velvet costumes bedecked with these pansies and little knitted woollen cardigans with scraps of Ophelia's speech stitched in the back.

At some point in 2007, Toti and I had visited Hungary. I had also bought a book in the Borzoi bookshop in Stow-on-the-Wold about world horse cultures. There were some glossy spreads showing the indigenous horsemen of Hungary, the Csikós (meaning, roughly speaking, cowboy in Hungarian). There were photographs of boys on well-bred bay horses galloping across the open Hungarian plain, the Puszta, wearing long blue indigo robes, standing up on their horses with a foot on each. In other photographs there were groups of these Csikós standing around watering wells with herds of horses, or they

were sitting beside their horses while their horses lay down. The boys looked calm and in control, the horses relaxed; an ancient agricultural world, little low houses, wide open plains, grazing cattle.

I did more research into this Hungarian horse world. The Hungarians are famously good horsemen. The country is made for horses – good grazing, flat, open. They excel in carriage driving worldwide and have a number of influential, quality breeds of their own, such as the Hungarian light draft horse the Nonius. Descendants of Genghis Khan, the Hungarian horsemen traditionally worked on the great plains, herding and tending horses, alongside their fellow stockmen – cattlemen, and in descending order, sheepmen and

pigmen. The horsemen are at the top of the hierarchy. The Csikós have two training specialities. The Hungarian Post, in which they ride two horses at once and drive any number in hand simultaneously, comes from the days of warfare when they would have to move large numbers of horses across the Puszta as back-up supplies. They also train their horses to lie down, providing the Csikós a place to hide, to conceal themselves, in the wide open plains.

The biggest of all the Hungarian plains was, I read, in the east of Hungary called the Hortobágy. The Hortobágy Puszta is a National Park and World Heritage Site. Hungarian legend says that it was created from a handkerchief thrown down by God for men to play on. In the boiling

Full swing. (Andrew Rees)

hot summer a mirage effect would sometimes reflect the image of the Csikós, blue robes flying, onto the huge skies. We had to go there.

Toti and I flew to Budapest, where we stayed at the crumbling Hotel Gellert on the banks of the Danube. We spent a day sitting in the vast ancient steam rooms and volcanic waters of the hotel, and then headed out by train to Hortobágy. It was very hot. Early summer for England but they were already well into haymaking. The train crossed an endless flat landscape. Little farmhouses, old tractors, lots of horses. We arrived at a tiny train station in the middle of the plain. We walked from the station to Hortobágy, were there is a huge red-brick hotel and massive equestrian yard. It is the home of the Hungarian National Stud. It was very quiet, and very hot. Yellow grass and dust punctuated by bright red geraniums. Hungarians love geraniums. We checked in and swam in an indoor pool. Later, we walked across the dusty track that ran between the hotel and the farm. There was just so much space, so much entirely flat open ground. Lots of very big outdoor schools. A whole string of big low barns, about a mile or so long. Some Csikós rode past, throwing up dust, chatting quietly together. A cart pulled by four brown horses and full of tourists rumbled past. Nothing was being done at a fast pace. There were no cars, no fences, no wires. There was nothing to startle and snag a young horse, nothing to get caught on, nothing out of the ordinary. I began to understand just how important country is in producing horses. It felt like you could do anything there. We walked along the barns. There were big stork nests at the top of telegraph poles. Rows of thatched barns with eaves that dropped down to the ground. In the distance, tractors were haymaking. Swallows swooped in and out of the barns. Toti and I looked into the cool darkness of the barns

and saw rows of mares standing quietly in stalls eating hay while foals played together in the wide open expanse of the barns. Slow time, hot sun, cool barns, quiet animals.

The hotel was more or less there to accommodate visitors to the National Stud. It wasn't exactly a thronging tourist destination. The Puszta World Heritage Site was full of rare birds and wildlife, so wandering about on it was discouraged if not actually forbidden. There were carts that trundled daily out onto the Puszta so that the curious could look upon the grazing ivory-coloured long horn cattle or the furry Mangalitsa Hungarian pig – the tourists were mainly Hungarian and a few German. I rode one day on a hired horse, and on another day Toti and I took the cart along with the tourists. The second day we were there, the hotel filled up with red-faced men and their families. They looked like farming families. Great bubbling cauldrons of goulash were set up on the terrace and there were tables laden with beer. The children of these families practised archery to the approval of their parents. They didn't seem to mind us being there, and Toti seemed delighted with the proceedings and very interested in the tractors. We had, without realising it, gatecrashed a John Deere new product launch, and Toti was in his element.

Some Csikós riders attended the event. They showed us how they got their horses to lie down and did the Hungarian Post. We tried to talk to them but our complete lack of any Hungarian was proving to be a real barrier. Hungarian is a difficult language. It is not Romance, Latin or Slavic, but is a member of the Uralic language family. It is impossible for a Hungarian to understand one single word of English without instruction, or vice versa. The Csikós seemed hot and bored. We absolutely failed to engage them at all, in any way. I remember talking to a woman who helped run the tourist programme at the stud. I could not get her

Opposite above: Set making – Jacqui Harrison. (Andrew Rees)

Opposite below: The band. The boy on the violin is Clover's son, Jimmy Joe. (Andrew Rees)

Left: Attila, a Csikós, a Hungarian horseman. (Andrew Rees)

Above: The subconscious throws up another reference – illustrations from a book that my mother used to love, *The Good Master*, set in rural Hungary. (Giffords Circus collection)

on my side either – I was boiling hot and feeling increasingly frustrated that I could not make myself understood.

We came back to England with no Csikós contacts. We knew not a single person in Hungary and I did not know what to do. I had a vision of a Csikós in his fine blue robes galloping across Minchinhampton Common, and I could not let it go.

Some time later my sister gave me an old children's book called *The Good Master*. My mum used to read it to us and she loved it. It is set in rural Hungary and is precisely about this world of the Csikós riders and families.

A series of coincidences then followed over the next year. We did actually return to Hungary and went back out into the provinces. Later in 2007 we attended a strange solstice festival on Margaret Island in Budapest, which was a coming together of lots of Csikós and Hungarian horse enthusiasts to drink beer, camp, eat goulash and practise archery. Archery is very popular in Hungary – you can become famous for mastering the backward shot over the shoulder, the Partheon or 'Parting' shot. We saw lots of Csikós, men playing polo only

with a goat skin, wild Hungarian gymkhana games, and we saw lots of archery, some of it mounted. The weather was hot and we were with friends – but still we made no contact with a Csikós. The language was still a problem and, I think, our credibility. I have learnt that Hungarians love Hungary with a passion. They love the weather, the boiling summers, the snowy winters, they love their plain food, they love their culture and consider it the best in the world. I have never met a Hungarian who doesn't consider Hungary the centre of the world. They certainly were not going to discuss giving it up to two strangers who didn't even speak Hungarian.

By chance, later that year, Toti's mother travelled with some friends to Hungary and she talked to someone there, an English man, who knew a man who ran a big driving establishment. She gave me this contact. I called him and he said he could help. He put me in touch with the son of his friend's head groom, a young trainee Csikós called Gabor. Gabor and his Swiss girlfriend then came over to England and stayed with us for two days. I spent this time with them, looking at our set-up

and discussing horses. We drove down to Cheltenham Racecourse where Edward Gillespie kindly met us and we looked at the famous track. Gabor said that he would like to work in England, and I said to him that if he found a Csikós willing to join us and do the season then I would help him meet more people working in the horse and leisure industries. He seemed a bit dubious, and certainly not prepared to take on the season himself. He and his girlfriend went back to Switzerland, promising to send me a contact for possible Csikós riders.

It was incredibly frustrating. I did not hear anything from Gabor at all. I was working on the new Caravan show in more and more detail. Toti and I imagined a scene with Ophelia's madness and the horse lying down. The Hungarian horseman, the lying down horse – they were both vital for our show. And yet impossible to find.

I gave up on Hungary. The winter passed. We bought a small black-and-white horse called Dominoe that I broke, and every week Tweedy would come over and we would practise in the barn together. It was a skeleton crew. We made progress with

Above: The Aloshin Troupe and their Rizley act. (Andrew Rees)

Dominoe – we would have a little riding act at least.

In the early spring a melancholic Frenchman came to work with us. He brought with him his small bay horse. I think he did not like our set-up at all, and left very quickly. Before he left, however, he said that he would like to sell us his horse.

'There is something about him I have not told you,' he said. 'He has been trained to lie down.'

Two weeks before we started Caravan rehearsals the thirteen-piece French brass band La Fanfare Suivante arrived in Bristol airport, singing, with their brass instruments slung around their necks, then proceeded to sing and play loudly all the way up the M5, giving me a severe panic attack as I was driving the minibus; I am not the most confident motorway driver, let alone with thirteen French singers bouncing around in the back. We were soon joined by a total of seventeen Russian gymnasts. Nancy was going to play the gypsy storyteller, painted from head to foot in gold. Bibi and Bichu were back, and were going to wear gold mesh and juggle knives and fire.

But we had one major problem. We still did not have our horseman, or indeed anyone at that point running the stables. I needed someone to run the stables – to train the horses, look after them and muck out. More than that, I needed an iconic horseman, a central figure in the show, someone to fall in love with. We had the little black-and-white horse, and the brown horse that could lie down, but we needed a proper rider and trainer, someone to work with the horse and be his friend. We had two weeks to go and we still did not have anyone. I put an ad in *Horse and Hound*.

I needed an iconic horseman, a central figure in the show, someone to fall in love with.

I sent Gabor an email. The odds of finding anyone seemed impossibly long.

During this time, Tweedy gamely said that he would come and help me full time in the stables. We were so busy by then, people were arriving, and I desperately needed someone to help me there. Tweedy was then, for a week or so, thrown into the position of yard manager. I did occasionally find saddles on back to front.

The start of rehearsals was literally days away. Molly was on her way from Paris. Still no horseman. Then I got a phone call. It was from Gabor. He said that he had found someone. He said he was called Attila and that he lived in rural Hungary and might be able to join us. I called Attila.

A man's voice answered but we were back to the same problem. He could not speak English and I could not speak Hungarian. In total desperation I called my one and only Hungarian contact, a saxophone player called Csuba. He worked on Circus Roncalli. Miraculously, I got hold of him.

'Csuba, listen, it's Nell. I am so sorry to call you out of the blue but I need your help.'

I explained everything to Csuba and, being the kind-hearted, helpful Hungarian soul that he is, he printed out a contract I emailed to him, drove all the way across Germany and Hungary that very day, met Attila, vouched for us, reassured Attila's wife that everything was all right and that me and Toti were good people, translated the contract and bought Attila a return ticket to Birmingham airport. Finally, and at the eleventh hour, we had ourselves a Csikós.

I met Attila off his flight at Birmingham. I didn't know what he looked like and he didn't know what I looked like. I stood at the arrivals gate, watching people wander, stroll, march and run past. I knew that I would know him when I saw him. The flight was delayed and I stood there for an hour. So many people passing by. And then there he was, a short, shy man, with a far-away wistful look in his eye, a questioning face, a springy step and a small amount of luggage and outdoor clothes. He was the horseman we had been waiting for, and from the moment I saw him I held him in the highest regard.

It was Molly who had insisted on a pre-rehearsal programme of production meetings, and when the rehearsals started she commandeered some of the startled art interns as assistants, and quickly trained them to jog behind her wherever she went, making notes. She installed herself in the top mezzanine office and without hesitation took hold of the control panel. She drove a system of meetings and schedules which meant that the art department in the barn, the horse department, the musical directors (Faith and Sarah, who were looking after the unruly Fanfare Suivante), the performers, and stage manager Ian Rumbelow were wired into each other in a daily flow of information. She is a brilliant choreographer who can direct, and direct she did.

We broke the show down into a series of acts linked by 'crowd scenes', each act and crowd scene encapsulating a different moment of the fair. One scene a storyteller, another the putting out of washing, another a meeting of people, another a horse sale, the Shakespeare vignette, and so on. Molly established very quickly a system of naming each scene and act so that they could be referred to in meetings and all present would know which bit of the show we were talking about in a heartbeat. Each

scene had an accompanying set of documents listing all participants, props and costumes, as well as light and sound cues. She taught one of the interns, who was by now on a fast track to running what must have seemed to be the biggest musical in the western world, to note down each and every movement in the show, an exercise towards producing a book of the show.

Whereas before Barry had worked on the movement of the finale and some of the individual characters, Molly, I realised, was going to choreograph *every single step* in the show. The cogs of Folly Farm were whirring. In the stables Tweedy handed over the yard manager job to Attila, who for a moment thought that Tweedy really was the horse master, and politely gestured for Tweedy to inspect his standard of mucking out. In the art department, the main barn, the students were painting 10-foot-high canvases to look like an old Victorian show front. One of the paintings was of Attila himself, galloping across a Cotswold landscape. Curious and silent, Attila inspected the painting. He kept walking back to the art department to inspect progress of the painting, nodding, smiling and saying 'Scheun scheun'.

Attila was entirely effective with the horses. They loved him. He took the Frenchman's little brown horse into the front field, which he called the Puszta, and galloped around cracking his whip, his Hungarian *karrakesh*. The brown horse reacted with some surprise at the loud crack of the *karrakesh*, and galloped about, bucking. Within an hour Attila was standing up on the horse, cracking the whip, while the brown horse, transformed, stood quietly beneath him. Later I explained as best I could that we would like the horse to lie down, which I found out that Attila referred to as 'Schlafen' (a few German words were our only common language). I tried to explain that there would be some people acting out a scene from Shakespeare

at the edge of the ring. Attila seemed to understand. He kept saying '*proba proba*' to himself and I found out that this meant 'try' in Hungarian. That was one of our key words. Try. Let's try it. I taught him the word 'maybe' and this was useful, because much of rehearsal is 'maybe' and 'try'. It is a picture on the page and this picture must be lifted from the page to the stage. The process is uncertain and experimental. Luckily for us Attila was made of stern stuff – he was what a theatre company needs, someone who will look for a solution not a problem.

The barn was full of painters and the tent was full of artistes being orchestrated by Molly. Wagons were being built in the workshop. The two costume rooms were full of girls hand sewing and machining – thirteen musician suits in linen and velvet, like a pack of cards, were coming to life.

This business of getting the vision from the page to the floor was something that I was learning about all the time. Earlier in

the year I had met with Barry at the Royal Academy to talk to him about Molly Molloy and to get his blessing on the new show. He was of course entirely gracious about this change in the creative team. But he had something to say to me.

'I think,' he crackled, 'that your pictures and drawings are very beautiful. But you don't get them off the page and into the design of the actual show. You must work much harder to make sure that you don't leave all your good work in your drawing books.'

He was completely right, and I realised with some disbelief that I had been doing exactly that. I had been working away at my drawing books and when I had achieved a satisfactory design, something at the back of my mind told my conscious mind that the job was done. But of course it wasn't. In fact, if the design work did not make it into the show then in a way it was pointless.

Barry's words rang in my head as we put together the Caravan show, and I think it was the first truly beautiful and unified show we had done. I tried to stick to a colour pallet of every version of brown from cream to gold. I thought about the fabrics of the agricultural fair – tweed, corduroy, wool, hessian – and used all these fabrics and only these fabrics in the costume and set. There were pansies everywhere, all around the outside of the seats and the ring and on the front of house. This worked really well, because the last scene was a wedding, and the tent suddenly felt like a wedding tent at a country fair, festooned with wild flowers. The bear, after endless trips to a workshop on the M25 somewhere, finally stopped looking like a kind of 1980s Huggy Monster and looked like a real brown bear. A photograph of it on our website triggered an investigation from the Department for Environment, Food and Rural Affairs, who had heard that we had 'illegally acquired a small brown bear'. The students of La Fanfare Suivante, with typical energy and a very high level of painting technique, helped us by painting the back boards of the tent – detailed scrolls and figures. It was beautiful.

Within three weeks of non-stop rehearsing we had a complete show. It was very good. Perfectly rehearsed, each and every move choreographed. Attila, a lost soul at an English horse fair, wandered around the ring leading a donkey and talking in Hungarian. There were energetic Russian acrobats, Bibi and Bichu juggled fire, Tweedy stood up on Dominoe in a billowing tweed coat playing the trumpet. Claire, the French chanteuse, sang Ophelia's madness speech.

And will he not come again?
And will he not come again?
No, no, he is dead:
Go to thy death-bed:
He will never come again.
His beard was as white as snow,
All flaxen with his poll:
He is gone, he is gone

And we cast away moan:
God ha' mercy on his soul
And for all Christian souls, I pray God.
God be wi'ye.
I hope all be well. We must be patient: but I cannot chose but weep, to think that they should lay him i'the cold ground. My brother shall know of it: and so I thank you for your good counsel. Come my coach!
Good night, ladies: good night, sweet ladies:
Good night, good night.

Nancy's face was painted gold, Claire sang, the band played mournfully. Ian Rumbelow spoke his lines as the 'Gentleman':

She speake much of her father, says she hears there's tricks i' the world; and sighs, and beats her heart.

In the middle of the ring the brown horse calmly lay down, as the *karrakesh* cracked.

At the end of the show Attila rode on, through a bower of flower arches, and married one of the musicians who wore a red dress while the cast carried a wedding feast into the ring, dancing and hanging garlands of flowers all around the tent.

The show tickets sold as fast we could print them. It was one of the wettest summers on record, and we finished the show in a waterlogged meadow on the outskirts of Cirencester. We were there for two weeks and the mud was historic – the wagons sank, the field flooded. People had to wade through water to get to us. There is a garage on the edge of the site and I could see people climbing along the railings of the garage to keep out of the water. But it did not put them off. Every day we had to lay three huge round bales of straw for the public and performers to walk on. The back tent was full of straw, the stables were full of straw. We pumped water out of the back

tent twenty-four hours a day and La Fanfare Suivante built a canoe to get around.

I can only be grateful to Sarah Westlake, the lovely lady who owns this meadow – we turned it into the Somme that year, and she only laughed, encouraged and helped us. The company did not flag for a moment. Permanently wet costumes, leaking bunks – we all began to feel amphibian by the end of that season – but nobody complained. The Fanfare were brilliantly ebullient. Attila cooked goulash for everyone. The Russians were Russians – inscrutable, vodka-fuelled, lighting their barbeques as if we were all in the south of France. It was a majestic year. The last day of the season was a lone fine day in a summer of rain. The sun shone brilliantly over the steaming marsh-like ground. Performers, musicians and crew all came out from damp bunks to sit on their steps and dry themselves in the unexpected sunshine. The strange atmosphere of the last day of the season hung in the air, that mixture of relief, heart-rending sadness and a nostalgic end-of-term feeling. Then something odd and magical happened. The Red Arrows – the Royal Air Force display team – flew over, trailing pink smoke behind them. They proceeded to draw a huge red heart in the sky, right above the circus, and then disappeared over the horizon. The red heart remained, suspended above the circus, melting silently into the blotting paper of the bright blue sky.

The 2008 company. (Andrew Rees)

LION HEARTS

We finished the 2008 circus season, Caravan. The continuous mud had made that last venue feel like a battleground. The company trouped back into Folly Farm like an army at the end of a campaign – everywhere there were piles of wet clothes and tents and muddy boots. Toti spent a week digging wagons out of the mud and they trailed back into the farm mud spattered and looking as exhausted as we felt. I cooked spaghetti and cheese non-stop for two days, turned up the heater in the house and put a sign at the entrance to our yard off the track saying that there was food for everyone in the kitchen. For two days the house was full of tired people, who just sat in the unexpected dry and warmth of the house dozing, talking quietly, eating spaghetti and sleeping. A strange Christmassy feeling filled the house.

We did not tour in 2009 and on 7 January 2010, in heavy snow, midwinter, another miracle happened: I gave birth to twins, a boy and a girl. We called them Cecil and Red.

Mrs Marinoff's sister-in-law, Daniella Ghionea, agreed to be the twins' nanny. She has helped me with them ever since and, in short, Dani is like a mother, to me and to them. I don't think we could continue to run the circus without her.

Above: Toti and Cecil. (Nell Gifford)

Left: Cecil and Red with Daniella during rehearsals. (Nell Gifford)

Right: Me and Red. (Giffords Circus collection)

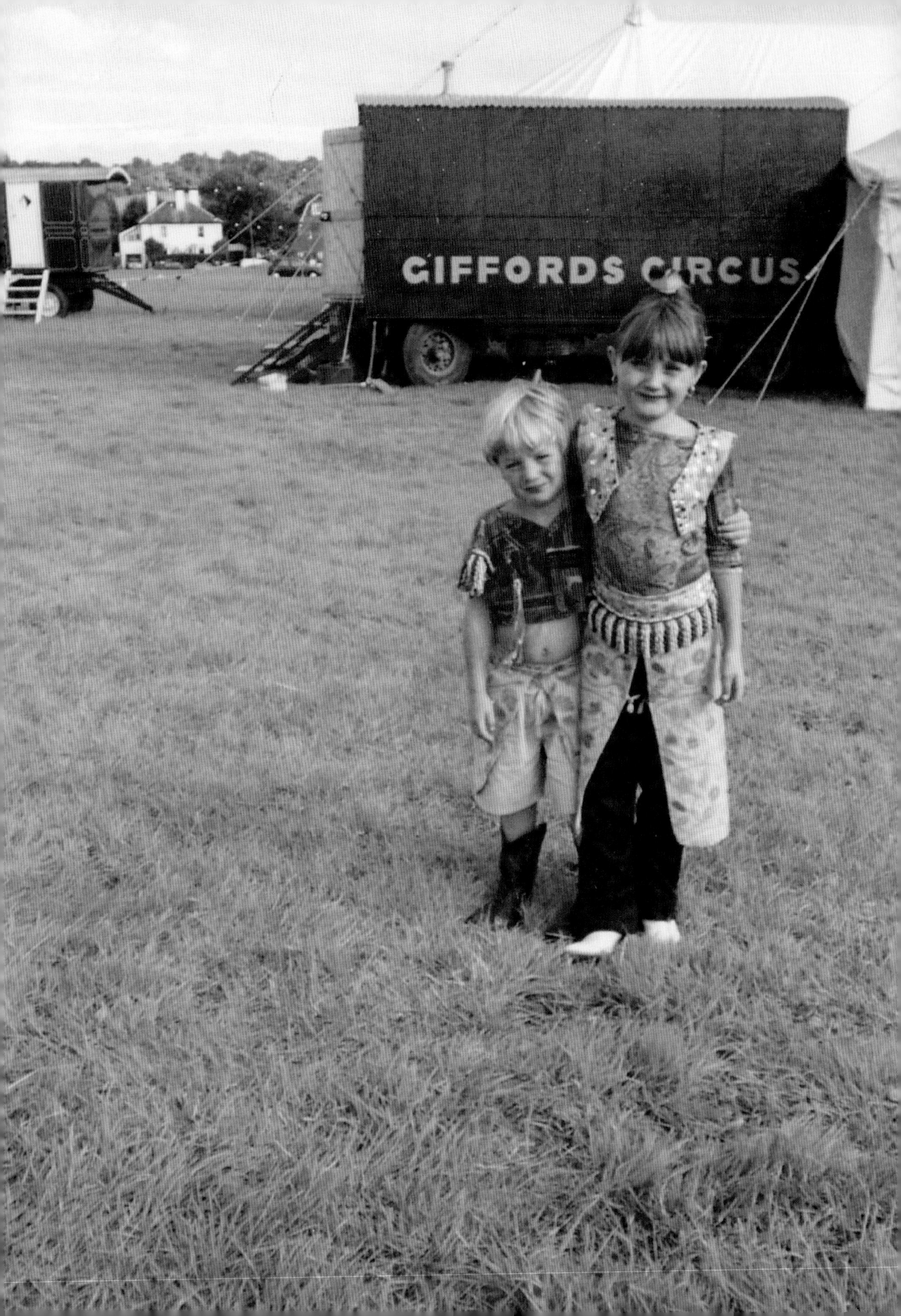
GIFFORDS CIRCUS

12

BRINGING IT HOME
CIRCUS CHILDREN

When I joined the circus in America I was 18 and my childhood home had ended due to family circumstances. I think that the circus was for me in some ways a new family and a new home.

Over the years, Toti and I have produced a lot of different shows for Giffords Circus. What I keep noticing about them is that without fail they seem to throw up, and in some ways manifest, some lost fragment of childhood. So the circus is, amongst other things, a representation of my childhood.

The circumstances of my mother's accident meant that there was not a maternal home to go back to, for Clover from the age of 16, for me from the age of 18. This is a specific though obviously not unique circumstance.

Bibi and Bichu's story intrigues me because they came to England at roughly the same age as I first went to the circus in search of something, and the language with which they describe their connection to us is familial – you were our family, they say, we had found our family.

Red and Cecil are our children, the children of Giffords Circus. But I don't think that they are the only children that belong to Giffords Circus, or who Giffords Circus belongs to. Over the years there have been a lot of children who have spent time here. My nephews and nieces have grown up with Giffords Circus. It is almost every day for them, for the older nieces Bibi and Bichu are almost their contemporaries. So the responsibility to run a happy show, a happy place, intensifies, because this is not a show – it is a childhood.

Left: Jimmy Joe and Rosa in our 2005 Cockerel Show. They had the responsibility of bringing the two tame bantams to the tent for the interval, a responsibility they rightly took very seriously. Rosa is a circus girl and she showed Jimmy the ropes a bit. They became good friends. (Julie Fossett)

Right: Rosa and Ian Rumbelow in the shop. (James Waddell)

This page: Toti and Jimmy Joe. (Andrew Rees)

Opposite above: Jimmy and Claudia Csilo, Attila's daughter. (Giffords Circus collection)

Opposite below right: Valeria Aloshin. (Andrew Rees)

Opposite below far right: Ivan Slipchenko. (Andrew Rees)

Right: Two Russian teenage gymnasts looking after 'Mrs Chicky', an adorable golden seabright bantam that my brother-in-law Matthew Rice gave me. She lived in the house and spent the evenings lying on Toti's chest while he snoozed in front of the telly. In the spring, when she loved being out in the barn, a fox killed her. (Andrew Rees)

Opposite above left: I look as if I have enormous number of children but they are nephews and nieces. The baby in the middle is Dolly, Clover's daughter. The little girl to the far left is my niece Elizabeth Rice, who is now a fully fledged circus performer. The boys in Stetsons are my nephews, Max and George Bridgewater, and the children at the front are Jimmy Joe Hughes, and Margaret and Michael Rice. (Giffords Circus collection)

Opposite far left: This is Rosa Fossett, from the famous Fossett circus family. They have helped us a lot and Julie Fossett is one of our circus godmothers. (Giffords Circus collection)

Opposite left: Claudia Csilo. (Andrew Rees)

Right: Nastia Kolomivets. (Andrew Rees)

EPILOGUE

I keep thinking that my parents brought me up to greet special occasions with enthusiasm and a sense of excess. Not financial excess, but an impulsion towards expending emotion and time on special events, and an imperative that special occasions should be homemade. I know that I had a privileged upbringing, and this is its greatest privilege. I think that Giffords Circus might possibly have never happened without this kind of early indoctrination into the importance of homemade fun, excess, and a sense that a special occasion should benignly disrupt.

This is what I have learnt – emotions must be moved by an event. Time should stop. If necessary, the traffic must stop. Special clothes must be worn and there will be music, lots of people, lots of laughing, usually a horse, and it must be made

Left: Me making preparations for the show. (James Waddell)

Right: Circus life – watching a football match on television in the caravan. (Giffords Circus collection)

at home, on the kitchen table. It might be a bit noisy, and it might make a bit of a mess – but who cares? The children can still be in bed early on a Sunday night and they won't be late for school, and everyone will help clear up the mess. Bunting will be taken down, fancy dress costumes packed away and the horse put back in the field. Emotional recovery might be a little longer, as you talk about the event with friends, look at photographs and contemplate that thing in your heart or your senses that has shifted that little bit. A joyful disruption.

I can see a slow death of the soul in only plugging in and switching on ready-made entertainment: a pre-packaged party, gliding seamlessly into a supermarket, gliding seamlessly into a shopping mall, gliding seamlessly into a ready-made packaged Halloween costume. I sometimes think that the English are forgetting how to celebrate and signify an occasion, in a turmoil of worries about getting it right and numbers and not inconveniencing anyone. I love the Caucasians' attitude to a birthday – total disregard for numbers, they just roll out the hot roasted meat and the homemade bread in vast quantities so that, beginning to end, people can feast and talk uninterrupted. Stop the clocks for a bit. Invite everyone and don't count. Dress up! Turn the sheets into ghosts! Pull the flowers from the hedgerows! Find some musicians! So the traffic goes slowly past the entrance to a fair, but for one day, does that really matter? Yes, the people camped by the side of the road leave a mess, and maybe they are gypsies or maybe they are young runaways and yes they look a bit dirty – but who cares? Live and let live; allow disruption and allow your emotions to be moved, now and again. Don't bolt it all down until spontaneity, along with all our festivals and festivities, are driven away. It will be much harder, once they have gone, to get them back.

So that is the story of Giffords Circus. It's our hymn to homemade fun, excess and benign disruption. We want our show to move something in you, and to take just a little while to recover from. We want it and wish it and mean it with all our hearts, because it is everything we believe about life and art and love. Giffords Circus is what I would most like to find if I were driving along a road. It is what I stop for, and it is what I would make a pilgrimage for. It is how I travel backwards to a lost childhood and how I travel forward, with my family and my art in tow.

> Giffords Circus. It's our hymn to homemade fun, excess and benign disruption.

ACKNOWLEDGEMENTS

In 2000, when the UK circus industry largely scoffed at the idea of Nell and Toti taking out a circus, Gerry Cottle saw the show and said that he admired Nell and Toti Gifford for producing it 'with absolute commitment'.

In 2000, Miles Connolly helped us move the circus between jobs with his removal van. In the same year, Cameron Robertson helped pay the wages of the artistes by foregoing his own for a week. He was helping in the box office. In 2002, James Greenwood wrote out a cheque on the spot when he found us sitting in despair in our caravan having had to cancel the tour due to the foot-and-mouth outbreak. These are just a few of the overwhelmingly kind people who, in the very early days of Giffords Circus, before we were known, took an interest in what we were doing and helped us during some of our most difficult moments.

I have tried to thank everyone here who has helped us. I am sure that I have missed people off. If you are one such person, I am sorry. And thank you.

P.S. In 2013 Paul Porter lent me the backroom of his pub, The Fox Inn, with its peaceful riverside view, to write this book.

Abigail Ahern; Adam Waller; Adrian Stewart; Aimee Morgan; Aleksander Likin; Alex Strong; Alexander Kashlev; Alexander Lyakishev; Alexandra Pringle; Ali Mohamed Devu; Alice Wimberley; Alina Popa; Amanda Hambleton; Amelie Julliard; Andrew Bulloch; Andrew Hall; Andrew McKinley; Andrey Berezentsev; Angela de Castro; Angus Wood; Anita Kwasniewski; Anna Matthews; Anna Partridge; Annabel Robinson; Anne Newhook; Anthony Bradford; Antonia Salter; Arabella Pollen; Attila Csiló; Barry Grantham; Bean Benson; Bella Lyster; Beth Schofield; Bibi Tesfamariam; Bichu Tesfamariam; Bill Harbottle; Branko Ristic; Brendan Rock; Caitlin Downie; Cal McCyrstal; Cameron Robertson; Carolina Santos Read; Caroline Mann; Carrie Freiman; Catalin Zaro; Cecile Pages; Celia Mendizabal; Celine Biewesch; Charles-Henri Fertin; Charlie Holland; Charlotte Newton; Chelsea Moore; Chino Odimba; Chloe Gwynne; Chris Garrard; Chris Hayday; Chris Hayward; Chris Tomlinson; Christian Icu; Christine Bottine; Christophe Carrere; Claire Barbier; Claire Collier; Clare Barbier; Clemency Calkin; Clover Stroud; Colin Hazel; Colin Matthews; Courtney Stone; Cristian Marinof; Dagir Magomedov; Dan Dare; Daniel Cesar; Daniel Fort; Daniel Hilary-Jones; Daniela Ghionea; Dave Cross; David Hibling; David Insua-Cao; David Shirt; Debbie Lloyd; Dolly Hughes; Donna Grimaldi; Dorian Claridge; Duncan Green; Ed Davey; Edward Richards; Elena Berezov; Elizabeth Rice; Elizabeth Elliott; Ella Pearson; Emelie O'Connor; Emily Campbell; Emily Leonard; Emily Park; Emily Seal; Emma & Matthew Rice; Emma Hope; Emma Kempton; Endellion Lycett-Green; Ewelyn Marinof; Faith Eliot; Faith Ristic; Fanny Beguery; Fleur Darkin; Francesca Simmons; Francois Marietta; Freddie Holding; Freddie Machin; Gabi Winwood; Gabor Vosteen; Garance Louis; Gemma Fuller; Gemma Waggett; Gemma Wells; Geoff Bartholomew; Geoff Jones; George Merrick; George Streatfield; Gerald Balding; Geraldine Davis; Grace Doran; Hannah James; Hannah Tottenham; He Yuan; Helen Finch; Helen Owen; Henry Cole & Bros; Hjálmar Baldursson; Hussein Juma Mwamroji; Ian Haywood; Ian Rumbelow; Igor Stynka; Imre Bernath; Irina Brown; Isabelle Woywode; Iurii Karpliuk; Jacqui Harrison; James Dale; James Gibson; James Keay; James

Towler; James Waddell; Jan Soencksen; Jane Beresford; Jane Smith; Jane Webb; Jannah Warlow; Jean Goubert; Jennie Fogarty; Jenny McLoughlin; Jenny Reeves; Jess Gibbs; Jesse Benns; Jessica Warne; Jessie Gaskell; Jimmy Joe Hughes; Joan Grantham; Jodie Murphy; Joe Bear Smythies; Joe Swift; Joely Clinkard; John Fogarty; John Newborough; John Walton; Johnny Aldridge; Jonathan Holloway; Jules Sanderson; Julian & Isabel Bannerman; Julie Austin; Juliet Mackenzie; Kate Bradford; Kate Harber; Kate Knott; Kate Smythe; Katherine Townsend; Katherine Whittington; Kathryn Cleverly; Katy Kelly; Kelly Rumbelow; Kennedy Nyambu Chisau; Kirsty Hanlon; Kirsty Richings; Kit Hesketh-Harvey; Kitty Rice; Kwabana Lindsay; Lady Colwyn; Lance Edwards; Laura Kreifman; Lee Kendall; Lin Grist; Lindsay Pugh; Liz Davenport; Lotte Seal; Louisa Birkin; Louisa Gaylard; Louise Coughlan; Louise Marsland; Lydia Gifford; Lynn Furnace; M. Lee Park; Maia Keeling; Maisie Bagley; Maisie McArthur; Maksym Tsvietkov; Malcolm & Nora Clay; Marc-Paul Verant; Margy & Martin Wood; Maria Shickle; Marine Class; Mark Borkowski; Mark Davies; Mark Knopfler; Martha Webb; Mary Haywood; Matthew Driver; Maximiliano Stia; Michael Black; Michael Oprea; Micky Seadon; Midity Schimellis; Mike Beer; Miles Connolly; Mirco Antoniazzi; Molly Molloy; Mr Archdale; Mr Bence; Nancy Landry-Trotter; Nancy Wilson; Naomi Belton; Natalia Zhuleva; Natalie Bird; Natalie Demjen; Neil Grundon; Neil Richardson; Nicholas Hooper; Nicky de Neumann; Nicola England; Nikkitta Shannon; Noel Stewart; Oana Oprea; Oleg Teplitski; Olive Gregory; Oliver Garrard; Oliver Halas; Olivier Taquin; Omar Tarba; Pat Bradford; Patrick & Brian Austin; Patrick Luke; Paul Porter; Paul Sargent; Pavlov Troupe; Penny Callow; Pete Allison; Peter & Bridget Gifford; Peter Csilo; Peter Sen; Phil James; Philip Bernays; Phillip Kuznetsoy; Phillipa Grimes; Pietro Cardillo; Pip Ashley; Rachel Furlong; Ralph Taylor; Rebecca Thomas; Rebecca Townsend; Rhiannon Jones; Richard Hart; Rick Stroud; Rob Thom; Robbie Parry; Robert Mann; Rocky Stone; Rocky Tebiev; Rod & Shirley Pearce; Roger Matthews; Roger Trafford; Romeo Tebiev; Ron East; Rosie Bristow; Rosie Ireland; Rosie Jenkins; Rosie Moxham; Roxane Errin; Roxanne Icu; Ruby Gaskell; Rupert Lees; Rupert Lycett-Green; Ruslan Arvelodovich;

Ruslan Tarba; Sally & Ben Morris; Sally Gibson; Sam Alty; Sam Hales; Sammy Weaver; Sarah Banbury; Sarah Duddy; Sarah Llewelyn; Sarah Mcmorrine; Sarah Poxton; Sarah Schwarz; Sarah Wallace; Scarlett Alexander; Sefu Swalehe Dzila; Selin Sarialtin; Serhiy Nemtsev; Shaena Brandel; Shane Bagley; Simon Lovelace; Sophia Antoniou; Sophie Collins; Sophy Bridgewater; Soslan Beresov; Srdjan Petrovic; Stella Cecil; Steve Jewell; Steve Parry; Stuart Driver; Stuart Rowland; Suzie Trotter; Sydney Florence; Sylvie Marchegay-Gifford; Sylvie Mills; Tamerlan Berezov; Tamerlan Tsoraev; Theresa Gibson; Tim Beauegard; Tim Mascall; Tim Payne; Tina Blankson; Tizzie Prentice; Tom & Camilla Bridgewater; Tom Holding; Tony Evans; Tony Wait; Tori Lawrence; Tweedy; Ursula Georgeson; Valentina Aleshina; Valentine Chatalet; Valeriya Aleshina; Venetia Nathan; Vicky Pennel; Virgile Elana; Vladimir Eatwell; Volodymyr Potaychuk; Wayne Horlick; William Rye; Willow Digweed; Yang Rui; Yasmine Smart; Yurii Slipchenko; Zsuzsanna Nyul.

Academy Costumes; Aggreko; Airstream & Co.; Andrew Rees Photography; Ascot Structures; Auto Value 2000; Bailey Paints; Benson's Apple Juice; Bolli Darling; Bourton Landrovers; Bourton on the Water Post Office; Bridgewater Pottery; Bristol Costumes; Burger Star; Butler Sherborn; Caroline Groves; Chadwick Oven; Cheltenham Borough Council; Cheltenham College Junior School; Cheltenham Stage Services; Cindeford Artspace; City Works; Clarissa Astor Flowers; *Condé Nast*; Cotswold District Council; Cotswold Farm Park; *Cotswold Life*; Cotswold Trading; Craig Hamilton-Smith Garden Design; Crocodile; CSS Lighting; Darcy Brown; David Smith and Maria Hurst, Chatcombe Estate; Edward Wheel, Stoate and Bishop Printers; Elliot Loo Hire; Everyman Theatre; Farming & Wildlife Advisory Group; FMcM Associates; Folly Farm Waterfowl; Forest of Dean District Council; Fosseway Hire; Freedom Fence; G.E. Stone; Gifford Shooting; Gloucestershire Community Foundation; Gloucestershire County Council; Gloucestershire Dance; Gloucestershire Music; Gloucestershire Wildlife Trust; Hardware.com; Hartwell Farm Holiday Cottages; Heber-Percy Charitable Trust; Hilary Grout & Ashgrove House Nursing Home; Jacquiharrison.com; Jive Pony; John Martlew & Co.; Leckhampton Dental Clinic;

Lewis & Wood; Loo Hire UK; Lord Faringdon Charitable Trusts; Love Is All There Is; Made You Look; Mangan & Webb Saddlery; Mike & Lella Day, The Retreat; Mitsubishi Motors; Mrs Margaret Guido's Charitable Trust; Mudway Workmen Marquee Contractors; Naturechild; NFU Mutual; Noa Noa; North Wiltshire District Council; O'Connors Plant Hire; Orchard Press; Partridge Solutions; Peddlars; Power Electrics; Prontaprint, Cheltenham; R.A. O'Donnell Jewellers; Refinish Systems Ltd; Selvedge; Septic Tank & Environmental Services; Severn Print; ShickPics; Southwest Arts; Stacks Property Search & Acquisition; Steppes Travel Group; Stewart McGill, The Playbox Theatre; T.E. Gifford Landscapes; T.H. Whites; Tabitha James Kraan; Tales on Moon Lane; The Arts Council of England; The Balti Waller; The Bath Road Traders; The Black Horse, Naunton; The Circus Space; The Dream Factory; The Green Dragon Inn; The Halfway House; The History Press; The Jerwood Charitable Foundation; The Notgrove Estate; The Playhouse Theatre; The Sash Window Co.; The School of Physical Structure; The Summerfield Charitable Trust; The Unicorn Centre; The Windrush Vaulting Club; The Yellow-Lighted Bookshop; Tivoli Construction; UK Event Services; Upstairs at the Beehive; V.W.H. Hunt; Walker Machinery; Warm Air Heating; William Bartholomew Party Organising; Windpower Design Ltd; Wookey Hole Circus; Zycko.

Venues: David Smith, Pegglesworth; Herefordshire Council, Hope and Anchor; Lord Bledislow, Taurus Crafts; Malmesbury Town Council; Marlborough Town Council, The Great Park; Minchinhampton Committee of Commoners; Mr & Mrs B. Warren, The Trout Inn; Mr & Mrs M. Wood, Summerhouse Farm; Mr Clifford, Frampton on Severn; Mr G. Ratcliffe, The Exmouth Arms; Mrs T. Assheton, Longborough Farm Shop; Peter Florence, Hay-on-Wye Festival; Sarah Westlake, Stratton Meadows; Swindon Festival of Literature; The Brighton Festival; The Frogmill Hotel; Toby Balding, Fyfield Stables; Uffington Village Green; W.R. Wingfield, Great Barrington.

This book takes the
story of Giffords
Circus up to 2008.
The story continues
with tours in 2010,
2011, 2012 and
2013. At the time
of writing, we are
planning our next
show for 2014
– The Thunders.
(Andrew Rees)